The Practice of
Managerial Leadership

The Practice of Managerial Leadership

Nancy R. Lee

Library of Congress Control Number:		2006909620
ISBN:	Hardcover	978-1-4257-4142-6
	Softcover	978-1-4257-4141-9

This book was printed in the United States of America.

To order additional copies of this book, contact:
Xlibris Corporation
1-888-795-4274
www.Xlibris.com
Orders@Xlibris.com
32739

Contents

This book is dedicated to
Elliott Jaques,
friend, mentor, visionary.

Acknowledgments

I appreciate the time Elliott Jaques spent editing this material so that it accurately represents his ideas in a linear, simplified form.

I also want to thank my many colleagues and clients who have helped me to understand, explain and utilize Elliott's concepts, especially Charlotte Bygrave, Sandi Cardillo, Kathryn Cason, Rod Carnegie, Ken Craddock, Sue Croft, Carol Dolan, Betsi English, Linda Gloe, Sabrena Hamilton, Tim Hart, Janet Kelly, Fred Mackenzie, Fran Marshall, Joe Privott, Susan Schmitt, Terry Seigel, Thad Simons, Betsy Watson, Tova White and Ken Wright.

Nancy Lee
Longboat Key, Florida
2006

Preface

Shortly after he returned from his service as a psychiatrist in the Canadian Army in World War II, Elliott Jaques became one of a pioneering group of psychiatrists and psychologists at the Tavistock Institute in London. Their military experience led them into innovations in organizations.

Jacques was consulting in the Glacier Metals Company when an employee asked him why it was that workers like him were paid by the hour while the executives drew an annual salary. That question aroused Jaques' curiosity and led him to start investigating the possible replies. His search led to a 50-year creative quest that became a major re-thinking of human capability and organizational structure.

Jaques' investigation took him into many parts of the world. A major learning experience was his consultation with Rio Tinto Zinc, a mining company in Australia. The chief executive of that company, Rod Carnegie, quickly grasped the import of Jaques' inquiry. Together they fostered extensive consultation in that company which resulted in a systematic refinement of Jaques' thinking and the profitable reorganization of that giant mining company.

Meanwhile he was also consulting with private and governmental organizations in Great Britain and did extensive work with the United States Army. Together these efforts, his writings, and the stimulation of working with companies in different countries fostered his conceptualization of human effort in organizations.

His thinking was a monumental reformulation of the basis of human capacity and organizational structure, reflected in twenty books and scores of articles.

Jaques not only posited eight different levels of conceptual thinking among human beings but also elaborated the curves of that thinking over an adult lifetime. In turn, his conceptualization gave rise to a new logic for organizational structure, an area that had previously had no logic for organizational leadership and accountability.

His work early on aroused my own curiosity and I invited him to join me in weeklong seminars I was conducting for the Levinson Institute. I also introduced him to several of the companies I was working with in the United States and South America. Executives quickly discovered his sophistication about their organizational lives. However, it soon became apparent that their re-thinking would have to go beyond slogans, clichés and traditional practices to become familiar with Jaques' formulations. Once they grasped his creative logic, they recognized that his thinking was far beyond what was in the management textbooks.

Jaques, with the help of his wife, Kathryn Cason, and the author of this book, Nancy Lee, continued to refine his thinking about levels of conceptual ability and even began to extend his thinking to understanding how animals differed in their capacity to grasp complexity.

Because his work required his audiences and his readers to make a radical change in their customary thinking about organizations and managers, many were reluctant to undertake that change for themselves and others and gave up on the possibility of introducing his concepts into their organizations.

In short, Jaques' work requires readers to take the necessary time to grasp his innovation. It also requires radical change in how executives are chosen and companies are organized. Like all new thinking his work necessitates testing the applications in one's own organization.

But grasping complexity need not be an overwhelming task. In this book Nancy Lee, herself an organizational consultant long immersed in Jaques' conceptualization efforts, has made his thinking much easier to grasp. That, in turn, should make this volume highly useful to executives, consultants and graduate students who seek to make organizations more effective.

Harry Levinson, Ph.D.
Chairman Emeritus, The Levinson Institute
Emeritus Harvard Medical School, Clinical Professor of Psychology

Introduction to The Practice of Managerial Leadership

The material in this book describes the comprehensive set of concepts, principles, practices and procedures for the practice of managerial leadership called Requisite Organization. These ideas are logical and consistent and have been developed over more than 55 years by Dr. Elliott Jaques and his colleagues in 15 countries. The ideas have been tested and put into practice throughout the world through continuing consulting research work.

Dr. Jaques chose the term 'requisite' to describe this integrated theory of how organizations work best because requisite means 'as required by the nature of things'. The ideas contained in Requisite Organization theory and practice flow from the nature of things—the nature of people, the nature of work and the nature of the relationship between the two.

Organizations exist to get work done in order to achieve their goals. Achieving organizational goals requires an organization that is appropriately structured, competent individuals at each organizational level, and procedures and practices that facilitate the work. This book deals with organizations that employ people—managerial hierarchies where accountability is delegated down through the organization from the owners/board members. People are employed within these managerial hierarchies as individuals (not as teams or as partners) to do the work required.

The material that follows is largely focused on the role of the manager because that is where most of the guidelines are needed in order to accomplish the goals of the organization. It is the work of managers that determines the results achieved with the available resources. Requisite practices enable decisive, accountable, value-adding managerial leadership throughout the organization. There is also information on the roles and accountabilities of non-managerial subordinates. Each employee needs to understand fully his or her own role and the organization's structure and practices. All of the principles in Requisite Organization are intended to enhance trust between employees *in* the organization and between employees *and* the organization.

Trust and understanding are further enhanced in Requisite Organization by the explicit definition of commonly used business terms. These terms are generally ill-defined and ambiguous. Clearly describing requisite practices and procedures in a consistent language that everyone understands provides clarity about what should be done and how to do it.

This book is written for managers at all levels in organizations. It is meant to introduce the material contained in Dr. Jaques' books, *Social Power and the CEO* and *Requisite Organization: A Total System for Effective Managerial Organization and Managerial Leadership for the 21st Century*, as well as his series of seven video tapes about Requisite Organization. The chapters in the book are organized in a manner similar to the videotapes so that they can be used together, if desired.

Chapter One describes the Basic Concepts. Chapter Two deals with Human Capability, Chapter Three describes Working Relationships and Chapter Four discusses the Organization Structure required to establish work and functions at the right level in the organization. Chapter Five explains Management Practices and Chapters Six and Seven are case studies that illustrate the process of implementing requisite managerial leadership in two different organizations. Dr. Jaques edited the first five chapters of this book for accuracy in explaining his ideas.

The theory and concepts in this book are set out as a series of propositions to be considered. The use of these Requisite Organization principles in the practice of managerial leadership results in increased productivity and profitability and provides employees with the opportunity to use their capabilities as fully as possible in a healthy environment conducive to personal growth.

Chapter 1

BASIC CONCEPTS

The practice of managerial leadership based on Requisite Organization concepts provides a systematic and science-based approach to management. These concepts, developed by Dr. Elliott Jaques, provide a comprehensive and coherent theory with an integrated set of principles that enables organizations and the people who work in them to be fully effective.

The use of Requisite Organization concepts enables organizations to:

- establish clear accountability
- establish the correct number of layers in the organization
- place roles in the right layer
- fill each role with a person capable of handling the work in the role
- provide clarity of roles and the relationships between roles
- assign tasks appropriately
- provide effective management practices

Many of the concepts that form the foundation for understanding how to achieve a requisite organization are introduced in this chapter. The first section explores organizations in which people are employed and defines the managerial hierarchy. The second section describes the all-important relationship between managers and subordinates. The third section deals with the complexity of tasks and the level of work in roles.

ASSOCIATIONS AND MANAGERIAL HIERARCHIES

More than 90% of those who work in the U.S. and most modern industrial societies do so in organizations that employ people yet, until Dr. Jaques' work, there was no precise definition of what these employment organizations are. It is essential to have a clear understanding of employment organizations in order to structure the roles and role relationships in them effectively and take advantage of the differing levels of capability that people possess to carry out the tasks necessary to achieve the goals of the organization.

Associations

Organizations that employ people are one type of association. An association is a social institution where the members of the group come together for a common purpose. There are voluntary associations such as companies, trade unions and clubs, in which individuals have chosen to become members. There are also non-voluntary associations such as nations, states and cities, whose citizens do not have free choice of membership.

Employment Organizations

In an employment organization, the owner or the association of shareholders, through an elected governing board called the Board of Directors, hires a chief executive officer (CEO) for the organization. This person, in turn, employs other people to produce the organization's products and services. The CEO is held accountable by the Board of Directors for the output of the employees. The resulting organization of employed individuals lacked a specific name. Dr. Jaques named it the '**managerial hierarchy**'.

The rights and obligations of those involved in a managerial hierarchy are defined in the legal charter of the organization. It is, therefore, useful to review an organization's charter and to understand the information it contains.

The Managerial Hierarchy

In a managerial hierarchy people are employed as individuals and have managers. The system of manager-subordinate roles that is developed from the CEO down through the organization is a hierarchy of working relationships. This hierarchy is a system of roles in which an individual in a higher role (manager) is held accountable by his/her manager (or in the case of the CEO by the Board of Directors) for the output of persons in immediately lower roles (subordinates).

A managerial hierarchy is a vertical organization for getting work done, with clearly specified accountabilities. In a managerial hierarchy managers hold immediate subordinates accountable for using their best judgment and commitment in striving to get the assigned work done, as well as for the results of the work of their subordinates if they are managers. In this way work and accountability cascade down in successive layers and a system of organizational layers is formed.

Many people have trouble with the word 'subordinate' as it has some connotation of lower or inferior. However, subordinate is used in requisite work since there is no other precise word available in the English language. In fact, everyone in a managerial hierarchy is the subordinate of someone else, including the CEO who is subordinate to the Board of Directors. Hence all employees are subordinates, and some are managers as well.

Definitions of Manager, Accountability and Strata

Some of the precise definitions that aid in understanding managerial hierarchies are those for manager, accountability and strata.

Manager

The definition of **manager is someone who is accountable for the results of the work and the working behavior of others**. The operant phrase here is 'accountable for'. People can 'report to' any number of others about any number of things, but in order for an organization to function properly it is essential to be totally clear about who is 'accountable for' what.

The lack of clear accountability by whom, for whom and for what breeds politics, buck-passing, and game playing and makes for dysfunctional organizations. In a requisite organization managers are held clearly accountable for the results of their subordinates' work, for sustaining a team of subordinates capable of doing the work of the unit they manage, and for carrying out specified, common sense leadership practices.

Accountability

Accountability is a situation where an individual can be called to account for his/her actions by another individual or body authorized to do so. Managers in managerial hierarchies are persons who have subordinates and who can be called to account for the results of the work of their subordinates by their own managers.

Strata

Dr. Jaques gave the term 'strata' to organizational layers. He selected the term because it describes and connotes a layer that is a band similar to a stratum of rock. The words stratum and strata will be used throughout the book interchangeably with layer and layers. In a **requisite organization strata comprise a series of layers in the organization**, with specified work of differing levels of complexity done in each stratum.

Other Types of Associations

There are other types of associations for common purposes including partnerships, churches, colleges and universities, doctors and hospitals and political organizations. The chief characteristic distinguishing these organizations from the managerial hierarchy is that their primary output is not generated by means of manager-subordinate relationships. Only the administrative work of such associations is accomplished using the managerial hierarchy.

Partnerships

Partnerships are associations where a group of partners, often professionals such as lawyers, accountants or architects, decide they are going to work together. They form a partnership company, and the partners produce the output. They may employ technicians such as paralegals or draftsmen and also support staff to help them get their work done, but the primary work of the partnership is done by the partners, who are not employees.

Churches

Churches are another kind of association. Clergy are not employees of this association but rather are very special, ordained members. The employees of the church are the people hired in an administrative capacity.

Colleges and Universities

In a university or college, tenured professors are members of the university association. They are not employees, and the heads of academic departments are not managers because they are not accountable for the work of the professors in their departments. Universities do, however, have employees and managers in administrative areas who support the work of the professional educators.

Doctors and Hospitals

Doctors are not employees of hospitals to which they bring their patients for treatment. They are not subordinates of the hospital president or administrator. The situation is different in a health maintenance organization (HMO) where the doctors are employees of the organization.

Government Organizations

In a nation/state/city that is democratic all citizens/members are equal, and they elect a government. It is this government that employs people in a managerial hierarchy. In the U.S. they are called civil service employees.

Family-owned Companies

There are also family-owned organizations that are managerial hierarchies but where there are interpersonal issues that generally need to be taken into consideration and dealt with in addition to the normal concerns of a hierarchical organization. For example, some members of the family may be part owners, others part owners and employees, and others employees only. Things become even more complex where one family member is the manager of other family members.

Understanding the Differences

Most management theorists have not identified, nor do they distinguish, these different types of organizations from one another or from the managerial hierarchy. This results in broad generalizations that are frequently misleading. It also results in recommendations for structuring organizations that are often inappropriate and counterproductive.

Dr. Jaques defined the differences. This book focuses on his work with managerial hierarchies. He also did extensive work in defining principles relating to the other types of organizations described above that are beyond the scope of this book.

Purpose of Requisite Organization Theory

The aim of Requisite Organization theory is to discover and describe how to structure and staff managerial hierarchies and institute practices that will enable them to achieve the results determined by the owner or Board of Directors. The use of the principles in this theory enables employees to use their capabilities to the fullest extent, releasing human creativity and enabling the organization to do business with efficiency and competitiveness.

Creativity and innovation depend not upon downplaying or trying to eliminate hierarchy (which is inappropriate because that is how organizations are legally established), but upon the development of requisite organizations that enable employees to work together harmoniously and effectively.

Organizations are Systems with Process and Structure

Systems are made up of both the **processes**—the way things happen—and the **structure** in which things happen. Managerial organizations, like all systems, are a result not just of processes, which are the focus of most organization theory, but also of structure.

A foundational concept of Requisite Organization theory is that **there is a requisite (or right and natural) way to structure organizations based on the nature of things.**

In a managerial hierarchy, organization structure must be looked at separately from staffing considerations and from organizational processes. In creating an effective organization, the first step is to define the structure by determining what roles are needed to get the required work done and at what level within a stratum (organizational layer) the work needs to get done. Decisions about structure and whom to place in given roles are often intertwined, instead of first defining a role and the work to be done and then determining who should fill the role, to the detriment of the organization and the people in it.

In the concepts and principles of Requisite Organization, Dr. Jaques described both the structure and the processes for successful and humane managerial hierarchies. The requisite managerial system is set forth in a clearly defined, logical and scientific way. Organization structure is dealt with in detail in Chapter Four.

Organization Structure (Roles and Role Relationships)

Organization structure is made up of roles and role relationships within which people work together. These role relationships establish the boundaries within which people relate to each other.

All personal relationships go on within boundaries, even spouse/spouse, parent/child or teacher/pupil relationships. Without the background of expectations that are built into roles and role relationships, people do not know how to behave toward each other. Role relationships set the external framework of mutual accountabilities and the authorities that govern the behavior between the incumbents of the roles.

Far from restricting freedom, having clear-cut role relationships established that are understood by those involved is the foundation for setting limits. These limits give real freedom within which to act because the parties involved know what is expected of them. For example, persons with drivers' licenses (a limit) are free (within required limits such as having necessary minimum vision, being sober, etc.) to hurtle several tons of metal down roadways (limits) at high speeds (again, with limits). Without such limits, no driver would have any real freedom.

Role clarity with the limits defined and understood, coupled with clear accountability and authority, builds individual confidence and esteem and generates trust in the system.

Organization Processes (Practices and Procedures)

Organization processes consist of practices and procedures that enable the organization to function effectively. In a requisite organization key processes include such things as context setting, task assignment, coaching and appraisal. These processes are dealt with in depth in Chapters Three and Five.

THE MANAGER-SUBORDINATE WORKING RELATIONSHIP

The most important relationship in a managerial hierarchy is that of manager and subordinate. Managers are persons in a role in which they are held accountable not only for doing their best personally but also for the results of the work and the results of the working behavior of their subordinates. Contrary to much management theory, managers cannot delegate all of their work. They have substantial work to do that is their own, including the work of managing others.

Managers are accountable for selecting qualified subordinates who are capable of performing the work required of them and for overall unit/department results. They are accountable for building and sustaining an effective team of subordinates and for carrying out the required management practices.

Managerial Authority

In order to be held accountable for their work as managers, by their own managers, there must be certain minimum authority with regard to immediate subordinates, including vetoing appointments, deciding upon a subordinate's removal from role, assigning tasks and conducting appraisals. Without such authority managers cannot be held accountable for the results of their subordinates' work.

Veto Appointment

Managers cannot be held accountable for the work of someone whom they do not believe can do the work required. Therefore, a manager needs to be able to veto the appointment of such a candidate. A manager does not need to be the person who chooses the slate of candidates for a position, that is done by the manager's manager.

A manager is not to be forced to accept someone as an immediate subordinate whom s/he judges cannot do the work in the role. It is usually the more competent managers who are asked to take on subordinates who are unable to perform satisfactorily, in order to help the company handle some kind of difficult problem. This is not a requisite practice.

Decide on Removal from Role

Managers need to be able to decide to remove immediate subordinates from their roles whom they judge are not performing at the minimum level of work required. Managers do not need the authority to discharge these individuals, since they are employed not by the manager, but by the company. But, if a given subordinate's work continues to be unacceptable after the manager has discussed the problem with the person and provided substantial, ongoing coaching, the manager needs to be able to tell his or her own manager that s/he no longer will keep this person as an immediate subordinate. It is then up the manager's manager (with the help of HR) to see if any suitable place can be found in the organization. It is the manager's manager who determines the need for separation from the company if no appropriate role is available.

Assign Tasks

Managers decide what tasks they will give subordinates to do. The manager's manager is not to by-pass the manager and give assignments, nor tell the manager what types of task to give subordinates or how to do specific tasks. That is up to the manager and is the manager's work.

The essence of the manager-subordinate relationship is the clear specification of the tasks to be carried out. Managers are also accountable for coaching their subordinates and providing them with ongoing feedback so they know how well they are doing.

Appraisal and Merit Increase

It is up to managers to judge how well subordinates are doing their work. Managers have the authority to decide, within policy, how much merit increase each subordinate receives. Leaving decisions regarding merit increase to managers higher up or to committees seriously undermines the immediate manager's authority and his/her ability to exercise effective managerial leadership. Each manager must be able to decide the personal effectiveness appraisal of immediate subordinates and decide merit pay within policy. The operant word here is 'decide': it is not 'recommend'.

Leadership

Leadership is a function of role. Some roles carry leadership accountability and some do not. Dr. Jaques designated the inseparability of the managerial role and the leadership accountability it carries by the term '**managerial leadership**'. All managerial roles in all functions in all strata carry direct leadership accountability with regard to subordinates.

Leadership is not made up of mysterious personality characteristics and charisma. There are not natural leaders who have certain inner qualities different from other people who do not have these qualities and, hence, are not leaders. Leadership is grounded in role and in the work of that role. The critical issues with respect to managerial leadership are an understanding of the managerial role and a knowledge of how to do the necessary work in the role.

Managerial Leadership

Managerial leadership is the process whereby the manager sets the purpose or direction for his or her subordinates and enables them to move along together in that direction with competence, full commitment and enthusiasm, dealing with obstacles they meet on the way.

Managers have the accountability to carry out established management practices with regard to their subordinates. This means that managers set direction and context for subordinates. They make decisions about whether subordinates will do their work independently or as part of a team. Managers provide direction in such a way as to ensure that they get their subordinates' full cooperation both with the manager and with each other. Managers need to win their subordinates' confidence in the managers' ability, in the managers' method of working and in the tasks they set.

Managers in roles in each stratum must have the necessary capability to exercise effective leadership in relation to immediate subordinates. They must be capable of doing the work in one layer higher than their immediate subordinates in order to carry out their managerial accountabilities such as providing necessary context setting, delegating tasks appropriately and making judgments of the personal effectiveness of their subordinates.

Misconceptions about Managerial Work

Managerial work is somehow felt to be contrary to the idea of effective leadership. There is sometimes a feeling that managerial work is autocratic, one-way down, and controlling. These are misconceptions.

The essence of leadership accountability is for managers to enable all of their subordinates to work together in such a way that each person can get on with his or her own work, knowing where all relevant others are going. In this way, everyone moves along together and the desired outcomes are achieved. A requisite managerial hierarchy enables the managerial leaders and the subordinates to move along together to achieve the organization's goals.

Subordinate Accountability and Authority

The manager-subordinate relationship is a two-way working relationship. Subordinates, too, have explicit accountability and authority. Subordinates are accountable to work to accomplish the tasks they are assigned and to bring to bear their full capability in working to achieve those tasks.

The basic nature of the employment contract is that **employees will always try to do their best to carry out tasks assigned by their manager.**

If a subordinate is doing his or her best, there is nothing more s/he can do to effect the results. The results are determined by the prevailing conditions and the decisions the manager makes in assigning tasks and resourcing them. That is why the manager must be held accountable for the subordinate's results, rather than the subordinate.

Subordinates are accountable to provide their managers with ideas and useful suggestions as to how the work can be done more effectively and for advising their managers if what is being assigned to them seems wrong or doesn't appear to fit the circumstances.

Subordinates are accountable to inform the manager if circumstances change while they are working to complete their tasks and if results cannot, in their judgment, be achieved as specified or if it is possible for even greater results to be achieved. This must be done in time for adaptive action to be taken. Working this way ensures that the manager is aware of what is going on at any given time and can adjust assignments as appropriate.

Individual Contributors

There is an important category of employees called individual contributors. These are people who work to complete the final output themselves. They can be found at any level in the organization, depending upon the complexity of tasks that they are assigned. Individual contributors may work alone or may have one or more persons assigned to them to assist in completing the work. In the latter case, the individual contributor is also a manager.

The role of chief economist in a bank is an example of an individual contributor role. This role would typically be immediately subordinate to the president of the bank.

Time Span and Organizational Layers (Strata)

Companies employ people to get the work of the organization done—work such as production, sales, bookkeeping, maintenance and so on. Yet until Dr. Jaques defined the term, there was no precise, generally understood definition of what '**work**' is. The lack of a clear understanding of what work is leads, all too often, to the situation where organizations become structured not for getting their work done, but for providing pay levels and career progression. Organizations then become structured in the form of grade levels for establishing status and pay brackets which leads eventually to the structure being decided upon not by accountable managers, but by human resource staff and job classifiers. Furthermore, the ability of a particular individual is often taken into account and the level or grade of a position is often raised to fit that person, rather than the organization structure being established on the basis of the work that needs to be done.

Such practices result in less than optimally functioning organizations and, in particular, cause a proliferation of unnecessary layers. It is the negative result of this excessive layering, with its attendant impact on productivity and morale, that so many organizations are addressing in their efforts at downsizing staff in order to survive in today's highly competitive environment. To correct the expensive and wasteful situation of having unnecessary layers, organizations are also eliminating layers of management.

Unfortunately downsizing is occurring and organizations are being flattened without any comprehensive model of how they should be restructured and why. In the absence of a specific definition of what work is, it is difficult if not impossible, to clearly specify the work needed to be done in the organization, to decide how many layers are needed, in what layer work needs to be done, and what roles and layers are no longer necessary.

Definitions of Work, Task and Role

The word '**work**' has many different meanings. Consider the following sentences: "That was difficult work doing the work I was given at work today. In my work I often have a lot of challenging things to do."

Here are four different uses of the word 'work'. The first connotes the effort applied, the second means tasks or assignments and the third indicates place of employment. In the second sentence the word work is used in a fourth way to indicate the role occupied.

In Requisite Organization practice the use of the word 'work' is limited to one meaning: **Work is the exercise of judgment and discretion in making decisions while carrying out assignments.**

In Requisite Organization there is also a precise definition for 'task'. **A task is an assignment to produce a specified output.** Tasks have a specified quantity and quality, and a targeted completion time. Tasks are carried out with allocated resources and within specified limits (policies and procedures). A manager assigns a task and the subordinate works to complete it.

Both tasks and the work that needs to be done to achieve them are distinguished from the 'role' someone occupies. **A role is a position in the organization.** Tasks are assigned to someone who is occupying a role in the organization. Using these definitions, the illustrative sentences above would be more clearly stated as: "That was difficult work doing the task I was given in my role of manager at the telephone company." The words 'work', 'task' and 'role' are used throughout this book with these definitions.

Work

The exercising of judgment in carrying out goal-directed tasks requires that the person understands the output to be achieved. The person either has been given a pathway to follow or has to plan a pathway to get to the goal. In either case, the person has continuing decisions to make and problems to solve.

If an employee is given a report to write and has been given three months by his manager in which to write it, what does that person have to do? He will have to decide what he is going to do, how he is going to do it, and how much of his time will be needed on different aspects of carrying out the task. Then more decisions are needed about exactly where and when to start, what references to look up, what literature to read. Next, decisions have to be made about what material to use and how to use it. All the time he is deciding whether to do this part of the task right now or do some other tasks that he has also been assigned.

Work consists of solving problems on a continuing basis. Organizations pay their employees for using their judgment in making the decisions necessary to carry out the tasks they have been assigned.

Task

Managers need their subordinates to work to produce certain outputs. They communicate a task (often calling it an assignment or goal or project) having in mind some kind of output that is expected to be generated when the task is completed—a report to be written, a research program to be completed, a table waited on, some calls on customers to be made, a sale to be closed. Output can be a finite product or a service rendered. Output, whether a product or service, is both visible and observable.

There are a number of parameters to each task that a manager must clearly specify including the quantity and quality desired, available resources and when the task needs to be completed. Any variance from normal policy or procedures also needs to be described.

Quantity (Q)

There is always a quantity involved in an output, hence the quantity needs to be specified or understood in the assignment of the task. It may be one, ten, or ten thousand. Examples of task quantity include: installing the dashboards on 10 cars; painting the trim on 100 specially ordered dinner plates; selling 10,000 barrels of oil.

Quality (Q)

The manager specifying output always has a quality in mind. There are always quality standards to be met. Too low a quality and the output is unsatisfactory; too high and more resources are used than necessary. The output needs to be provided within certain quality standards, and these standards must be set in terms clear enough that everyone knows what they are. If a subordinate is to produce a given quantity to that quality, it is necessary to make that quality understood.

Resources (R)

Tasks need to be assigned in terms of resources—the amount of money that can be spent, how many people can be used, what equipment and materials are available. To continue the example of the report that needs to be written, the manager assigning the task further states that books on the subject will have to be reviewed and a literature search carried out. She tells the subordinate that there is a budget of $900 to cover research expenses and provides the use of the summer intern to compile the bibliography.

Time (T)

What is often not specified, but always exists in the mind of the manager, is the outside time limit by when the task must be completed. This is the 'when' of a task. A task is not only a 'what' but is a **'what-by-when'**—that which is to be completed by a targeted time. The completion time that is targeted by the manager should be made explicit when assigning a task, or the manager should be confident that the subordinate understands the target completion time.

The time the manager has in mind when assigning the task by when s/he needs the task to be completed is called the 'target completion time'. The manager plans this target completion time to fit with the other tasks that the manager needs to get done toward achieving the department goals.

One of the reasons for making the time explicit when assigning a task is that the subordinate can discuss with the manager any problems anticipated in meeting that timing given the resources, quantity and quality specified.

In the example of the assignment to write a report, the manager stated that the researcher had three months to complete it. The manager did not want it in six months, but specified that it be completed in three months. The manager further expected the subordinate to work on this report along with other ongoing work in such a way that the report would be completed on time as well as all of his other assigned tasks.

There is an important point here that needs to be understood. If the manager assigns a task that is to be completed in three months, it is a different task than if the subordinate is given one month to do it, and again different if the time specified for completion is six months. Some people have difficulty with this point and think that it cannot be a different task just because the time allowed is two months less or three months more. But it is a different task, and the subordinate will need to make different decisions and behave differently.

With six months to do the report, the person assigned the task may choose to spend a lot of time at the beginning preparing very carefully, ensuring that all possible references have been discovered and reviewed. With only one month to do the report, the subordinate will decide to do much less research and the literature review may have to be much more cursory. The employee will have to decide priorities with regard to the work he has to do on other tasks in quite a different way, because of the allotted time he has been given to complete the report. Depending upon how much time he has to spend on the report, he will have to decide what can be set aside for now and what cannot, in working to complete all of his assignments on time.

Policies and Procedures

Organizations have company-wide and department policies and procedures. It is a manager's job to familiarize subordinates with these and see that they are adhered to in working on tasks. For example, the report must be no longer than 50 pages and must be bound in accordance with the standard procedure.

QQT/R

A task, then, can be defined as a quantity (Q) of things within given quality (Q) limits to be produced by a target completion time (T) within specified resource limits (R) or QQT/R. Although quality standards, resources and policy and procedure limits are not always explicitly stated, they always exist and are implicitly assumed by both manager and the subordinate. If no target completion time is assumed, it is difficult to plan and organize to get the task done.

The manager and subordinate can discuss any of these parameters to agree on an outcome that is satisfactory to the manager and that the employee believes can be accomplished as assigned. This is part of the two-way working relationship.

Context Setting

The manager needs to provide context for the subordinate by showing how the completion of this task fits with the other work that is being done and by describing the larger outcome the manager is seeking. "Hank, I need this report completed no later than three months from now since I have to put it together with the material that Sue and Jose are doing in order to advise the president on a recommendation to the board." It is this kind of context setting that enables subordinates to move along together with the manager.

As the task proceeds, clear context setting and specification of QQT/R enable the subordinate to evaluate the situation and make good decisions. If the original time frame was not realistic, the subordinate must advise the manager as soon as possible so that the manager can re-evaluate the task, the target completion time, and the resources needed. Or, if there should be a change in circumstances, the subordinate can come back to the manager and discuss the situation. If the subordinate can finish the task sooner than requested, the manager, once advised, can plan accordingly. By having this information, the manager can modify priorities and determine the results that will be achieved by the work of subordinates.

This type of feedback enables tasks to be done on time or revised as required. It also enables full use of employees' time and talent. It eliminates the game-playing often brought about by such practices as management by objectives, where subordinates often only agree to end results which they are absolutely sure they can achieve or where they intentionally overestimate the time needed for completion. The manager needs to know what actually can be achieved if subordinates use their full capability. Requisite practices enable honest estimates and continuing feedback as to progress. Realistic estimates and continuing communication and feedback in assigning tasks and working on them builds trust between managers and subordinates.

LEVEL OF WORK AND TIME SPAN OF DISCRETION

Comparing roles within an organization or between organizations has always been very difficult, if not impossible. There has been a great deal of concern in recent years about providing equal pay for comparable work. But how is comparable work to be measured? There has been no accurate way of talking about comparable work with regard to how complex the work is. This is an example of the problems caused by a lack of clear definitions of the word work. In talking about comparable 'work', the word 'work' is often used in seeking to determine comparability both in the sense of the tasks involved in a role, and in the sense of what a person must do in order to carry out the tasks.

Level of Work

Dr. Jaques used the term **'level of work'** to talk about the complexity of what needs to be done in a role in order to carry out the tasks that are given to that role. It is evident that the level of work varies from role to role, but how can this be thought about or described, and what is it that is being described? The level of work of a role is commonly talked about as the 'size of a position', 'how big one position is compared to another', 'how big a role someone has', 'how heavy the responsibility is in a role', 'the amount of responsibility in a role', 'the weight of the responsibility of a given kind of work'.

These ideas of more complex or more difficult or higher levels of work do not refer to more work in quantity but to work that is greater or lesser in scope. Although everyone has a sense of what these ideas mean, until Dr. Jaques developed and specified the concepts and definitions of Requisite Organization there was no clear, unequivocal language to describe or to discuss them.

Job evaluation schemes seek to measure differences between the level of work in roles, but they are unsuccessful. Current job evaluation measures are cumbersome, subjective and unreliable because they do not have a precise definition of what they are measuring. They do not have a clear concept of what it is about the work that varies in size. They, therefore, lack an objective method of measurement.

There is, however, a method of comparing the level of work in roles in managerial organizations that was discovered by Dr. Jaques as the result of the consulting research he was doing in organizations. This measurement is called the time span of discretion. It is also referred to simply as 'time span'.

In order to carry out this measurement it is necessary to note the distinctions between two types of roles:

- *Multiple-task roles,* in which the manager assigns numbers of short and longer term tasks, to be worked on simultaneously, and
- *Single-task roles,* in which the employees have only one task at a time to be completed before starting the next.

In both cases, employees have to balance efforts to assure that they are working both quickly enough and well enough to meet time and quality targets.

Time Span of Discretion

Every task has a time by when the manager wants it completed. Even when managers say they do not have such a time frame in mind, upon questioning it becomes evident that there is always a maximum time in their mind by when a task has to be completed. It is possible to observe and study the time frame—the target completion time—that a manager has in mind when s/he assigns a task.

Time Span in Multiple-Task Roles

In a discussion with the immediate manager of a particular role, a trained observer can discover which of the multiple tasks being assigned to that role have the longest target completion time. No one other than the immediate manager can provide this information because it is his or her decision. The target time of the longest tasks in a role turns out to provide an objective measurement of the level of work of a role.

These longest assignments give the longest time that the manager must rely on the judgment of the subordinate. This is because the subordinate can borrow against completion times of these assignments, in balancing pace against quality—that is, doing well enough, quickly enough.

Consider the case of a subordinate who has been given five tasks that need to be finished by the end of the day, another two that must be done next week and yet another that needs to be finished in two weeks. If the last task is the longest task the subordinate has to deal with, the time span of that role is two weeks. That is the measure of the level of work of that role and places it requisitely in a specific stratum in the organization.

Subordinates are given longer and shorter task assignments and are given additional task assignments from time to time. The longest task assigned is not necessarily the most difficult or most complex task in a role. However, it is the longest task(s) that a manager gives a subordinate that provides the measure of level of work in that role. This is because the subordinate must be capable of juggling the planning of and completion of all other tasks assigned to him/her in that role within the time frame of the target completion time given for the longest task.

Time span is an objective fact, since it is derived from an objective decision of the manager. Time-span measures cannot be falsified because managers are committed to the target completion times they set, and the effectiveness of these decisions can be checked by their managers.

The longer the time span of a role, the higher the level of complexity of the work in that role. Any two roles with the same time span, regardless of occupation, have the same level of work. Information on how to measure time span is found in Chapter Five.

Time Span in Single-Task Roles

In addition to roles that have multiple tasks that must be balanced against one another, there are roles that have single-task assignments. There may be a number of sub-activities involved in carrying out the task, but the full task itself must be completed before moving on to the next task. An example is the work of a batch-work machine operator who must complete each batch in its given order and by a specified completion time. Another example is a document clerk who must complete each document in order and by completion time. Most single task roles are first-line work.

There is an important difference in one-task-at-a-time roles and multi-tasks roles. In the latter, employees can borrow against time needed to complete other tasks if they cannot get any individual task done in a timely fashion as assigned. The manager may not know if the subordinate is doing this until some of the longer tasks fail to be completed.

In the roles where one task at a time must be done, the manager will know right away if the task is not completed on time, but may not know for some time if the quality of the work is not up to standard. For example, an operator may be working quickly enough, but the manager will not know if the output is of good enough quality until some of it arrives at the first point where the quality is checked. In this example the employee is, in effect, borrowing against the minimum acceptable quality of work in the role in order to appear to get the work done in the time specified. In single-task roles the time span is measured by the length of time it takes to determine if the work of a subordinate is just marginally sub-standard.

Origins of Time-Span Measurement

The evidence that, by itself, the time span of a role measures the level of work in that role comes from a number of sources. First is the accidental finding in 1953 by Dr. Jaques that individuals working at the same time span stated the same total compensation to be fair and just for their work, regardless of occupation, actual pay, or any other factors. These findings have been confirmed in 15 different countries since that time. Second is the consistent finding that if the time span of a role is increased, the incumbent feels the weight or level of responsibility to have increased and vice versa. Finally, there is the finding that time-span measurement reveals a universal basic structure of organizational strata for all employment organizations. This last point will be discussed in detail later in this chapter.

In the 1950's, Dr. Jaques was working in the United Kingdom at the Glacier Metal Company with a group of junior staff who were concerned with fairness. They asked him if he could help them get away from job evaluation jargon and find a direct way of measuring work so that the work one was given to do determined pay and status, rather than pay and status being based on one's social status and accent. After months of seeking a method of measurement to no avail, the group suggested to Dr. Jaques that it might have something to do with time, since the higher one went up in the system the longer was the period of time used to describe pay. Workers' pay was described in terms of hourly rate or a daily rate, then the next level up had weekly pay, managers got monthly salaries and pay for senior executives was talked about in terms of annual compensation.

While exploring this issue, Dr. Jaques found that the target completion time of the longest task or tasks assigned to a role seemed to indicate a difference in the complexity of the work in that role relative to other roles. He also discovered that there appeared to be a consistent and universal amount of pay that was felt to be fair for each of the different role strata and levels within the strata, as established by time-span measurement.

There appeared to be an important connection between the weight of responsibility in a role, the level of work in that role, and what people considered as reasonable pay for what they were given to do. (**Responsibility** in this case **is defined as something one is depended upon or trusted to carry out.**)

People working at the same time span talked about similar amounts of pay as being fair for work they were doing. This finding, which is referred to as 'felt fair' pay, has proven to be consistent throughout the years with regard to relative pay for various levels of work, in all types of organizations and in many different countries.

THE REQUISITE PATTERN OF ORGANIZATIONAL STRUCTURE

A pattern of work emerged that became the basis for evolving a requisite management structure for management hierarchies based on the discovery of time span and the proposition that time span gives a measure of level of work. This discovery was further confirmed by the finding that people appear to have a fairly universal sense of fairness of total compensation for given levels of work.

Dr. Jaques found a consistent pattern. Persons in roles with a time span below three months will describe as their 'real' manager whoever is in the first role that has a time span above three months. There may be shift supervisors or other levels and titles in between in roles that have time spans below three months, but the subordinate worker will not consider any of these people as their actual manager. They, of course, are not aware of the time span, but rather are aware of who really gives them guidance and direction.

This pattern continues in a regular and predictable fashion with the next breaks occurring at one year, two years, five years, ten years and twenty years. These are critical boundaries between strata. Individuals working effectively in a role with a time span of more than three months but less that a year will name the first person with a time span of more than a year as their real manager, no matter how many apparent levels of management there are in between.

In order to have effective managerial leadership, a structure of layering has to be set up with the first stratum—operators/clericals—in roles with time spans between one day and three months (if such work is needed by the organization), then the first-line managerial stratum between three months and a year. The next layer of roles, typically that of department managers, has time spans between one and two years. Managers of functions are then found in roles having time spans between two and five years, business unit presidents between five and ten years, corporate vice presidents between ten and twenty years and finally the chief executive with a time span somewhere between twenty and fifty years.

The time span of any given role that falls within one of these strata will fall somewhere within the range of that stratum. For example, one role in Stratum I (one day to three months) can measure one week and another role can measure one month. A role in Stratum II might measure six months or eight months. The objective 'measure' is the longest target completion time of a task that a manager actually assigns to a specific role. Wherever it falls is the level of work of that role.

The Requisite Strata Required

The findings described earlier with regard to time span and to 'felt fair' pay led Dr. Jaques to conclude that a business unit needs no more than five strata, a corporation consisting of more than one business unit needs no more than seven strata and a mega-corporation that is composed of several large corporations needs no more than eight strata.

These findings mean that multi-billion dollar companies employing perhaps 20,000 or 30,000 employees can operate effectively with only seven layers, from the CEO down to the shop or office floor. Where there are additional layers, one or more people will fall into the same layer and provide no value-added for the organization. In fact, there is value-subtracted, and this practice is counter-productive.

Not long ago many organizations had 12 or even 15 layers. It is no coincidence that in the face of tough global competition one of the first cost-cutting measures in many organizations has been to eliminate unnecessary layers in an attempt to become more effective and efficient. Organizations have a sense that there is no added value in many of these layers but, as was mentioned earlier, the difficulty is that decisions are often made in flattening or 'delayering' without any conceptual theory. This damages both organizations and their employees.

ROLE COMPLEXITY AND TASK COMPLEXITY

The complexity of a role can be objectively measured by the use of time span. It is not yet known how to measure the complexity of a task.

Role Complexity

The time span of and the complexity of a role, as measured by the longest task in the role, determines the organizational level at which the role should be placed. The longer the time span of a role, the higher the level in the organization the role needs to be positioned. There is, furthermore, an observable and consistent relationship between compensation for a given role that is felt to be fair and the complexity of that role.

Task Complexity

Although differences in task complexity cannot be objectively measured, it is possible to describe these differences. Managers, in fact, generally have quite a clear idea of the differences in the complexity of tasks. They are aware both of the differing complexity of tasks and the differing ability of their subordinates to carry out assignments. Managers use that knowledge every day in their planning and assigning of tasks and work.

What does the complexity of a task mean? How is the complexity of a task understood and described? The complexity of a task cannot be looked at in terms of the result that is to be achieved, that is, in terms of the output. Where is the complexity of a task if it is not in the output?

The complexity is found in what has to be done in order to get to the output. The complexity is in the pathway to the goal, in what needs to happen on the way to the goal. In studying the impact of gravitational force on a free falling body, there is no use studying the state or condition of the body after it has hit the ground. That is the result. What has to be observed is the process, what is happening as the body is falling. Differences in task complexity can be observed in the differences in the process involved in working to achieve a goal.

The complexity of a task is a function of the complexity of the work involved in doing that task. Task complexity can be studied and understood by looking at the pathway to a goal and describing the work involved—what has to be done to arrive at the goal, what judgment has to be used, what decisions have to be made. It is important to understand work in terms of its complexity and that as one goes higher up in work systems, the complexity of the problems to be solved increases.

Following are descriptions of pathways and actions of different types of complexity in the different strata in the organization.

Stratum I Complexity

In Stratum I, the manager assigns a task and describes the pathway to follow, telling the subordinate about the obstacles that can be expected and what should be done to overcome each one, if and when encountered. The subordinate is provided with a description of a specific pathway to the desired goal. Work in this stratum requires direct action and problems are dealt with as they are encountered. This process is called **direct judgment**.

The subordinate does not have to anticipate difficulties. When subordinates encounter an obstacle they use information provided by the manager to try to solve the problem. If the problem cannot be solved as the manager has described, or if other obstacles are encountered that the manager has not anticipated, the subordinate goes to back to the manager for direction as to what to do. The time span of roles in this stratum is from one day to three months. This means that a role at low Stratum I might have a one day task as the longest task in the role, a role at mid Stratum I might have the longest task at ten days and at a very high Stratum I might have a task or sequence of tasks as far out as almost three months.

An example of Stratum I work could be found in a commercial organization that makes photocopies, and the copies are not coming out dark enough. The copy machine operator has followed the manager's instructions about what to do in this event, which is to change the toner cartridge. If this does not fix the problem, the operator has to go back to the manager to ask what to do next.

Stratum II Complexity

Individuals capable of working at Stratum II are able to use diagnostic judgment in accumulating information and putting that information together to solve problems along the pathway toward a goal. This is the level of first-line manager and of individual-contributor analyst roles. At Stratum II someone has to be able to anticipate the relevance of particular items, to recognize what pieces of information are important in solving a problem and what are not. This process is called **diagnostic accumulation**. The time span of roles in Stratum II is from three months to one year.

An example of diagnostic accumulation is the work of detectives in solving cases. Clues are discovered and accumulated (or rejected as misleading or irrelevant) in order to reach a conclusion. Another example is an analyst's preparation of a report where information has to be gathered and conclusions arrived at, with numerous decisions made along the way about what to include and what to leave out.

Stratum III Complexity

Someone working in Stratum III has to be able to think out a number of pathways and choose the best one to follow. If the chosen pathway turns out not to be proceeding as planned, s/he needs to be able to change to one of the other pathways. This is called **serial processing**. This is the stratum of middle managers in the organization, and the work requires the ability to construct and to use alternative plans. The time span of roles in this stratum is from one year to two years.

An example of task complexity at Stratum III would be someone who is reorganizing the machine department in a factory. She has considered gradually training her operators section by section. She has also thought about training all of her operators at one time. In considering both possibilities, and perhaps even a third or fourth way of approaching the problem, she weighs the pros and cons of each pathway and makes a choice. If the chosen pathway does not succeed as anticipated, she then selects another pathway to follow.

Stratum IV Complexity

Stratum IV is the functional manager stratum where a person does not deal with just one pathway at a time, but manages numbers of pathways in relation to each other. This is called **parallel processing**. It is the kind of work that involves critical path analysis and where PERT charts are used. Assignments of Stratum IV complexity require that numbers of interactive projects be undertaken and adjusted to each other with regard to resources and timing as work proceeds in order to keep the total program on target. The time span of roles at this stratum is from two years to five years.

An example of the type of work at Stratum IV is found in the role of a general sales manager who has a number of subordinate regional sales managers working at Stratum III overseeing Stratum II sales representatives. All of their work and the available resources and changing conditions have to be balanced on a continuing basis in order to reach the company's sales goals.

Stratum V Complexity

At Stratum V, that of business unit president, the person in the role has to deal with a unified whole system. This role requires the use of direct judgment, but the information that now has to be used is at a higher order of complexity than the information used in roles at Strata I through IV. There are a wide variety of issues that have to be worked on in the context of the relationship between the business unit and the outside marketplace. This is where profit and loss accounting takes place. There are financial, human resourcing, production, technology and product research issues to be dealt with which interact with each other. The business unit president has to handle problems like shortage of raw materials, strikes, rising costs, new product issues and so on, playing the whole range of complex variables against each other. The time span of this stratum ranges from five to ten years.

Stratum VI Complexity

The roles of corporate executive vice presidents in large corporations are at Stratum VI. Here again is a diagnostic accumulation type of work but at a higher order of information complexity. Executive vice presidents are dealing not just inside the corporation but with issues involving the whole world-wide environment. Problems have to be anticipated that are concerned with external political, economic, and societal issues. The time span here ranges from ten to twenty years.

Stratum VII Complexity

The Stratum VII corporate CEO puts Stratum V business units out into society. This involves dealing with the complexity of financial market issues, of balance sheet value of the business units, of issues of major competitors and of what is happening in the world on a continuing basis. The time-span in this stratum is from twenty to fifty years.

Stratum VIII Complexity

There are some very large organizations, such as General Electric, that are made up of a number of Stratum VII corporations. The time frame here appears to be longer than fifty years. This type of mega-corporation has not been studied in detail.

Orders of Complexity

There is an increase in complexity of work and tasks as one moves up to higher and higher strata in the company. Discontinuous change in the complexity of the work required to accomplish tasks occurs at each stratum. These changes are not gradual but appear as if one moved from one step to quite a different step—from one way of processing information to a different way. There are distinct differences in how information is used in making decisions as one's complexity of information processing matures.

There appears to be a very basic relationship between the fact that there is a requisite structure for managerial hierarchies based on the complexity of tasks and the roles where those tasks are assigned, and the need for higher and higher levels of problem-solving capability. This appears to be based on and required by the nature of work, tasks and human capability. Differences in human capability are explored in Chapter Two.

Chapter 2

HUMAN CAPABILITY

The basic Requisite Organization concepts discussed in Chapter One, including managerial hierarchies, roles, work, tasks and structure, provide a clearer understanding of organizations in which people work. In Chapter Two the people who work in these organizations, these managerial hierarchies, are considered with regard to human capability and its use in working to produce desired results. The focus here is on an increased understanding of people at work, the differences in their capability to get tasks of differing degrees of complexity done and the maturation of this capability over time.

Requisite Organization principles and practices provide a total system of management, of organization structure and of how people work together. The use of this system results in effective organizations and effective circumstances for individuals to be able to use their full capability in their work.

THE NATURE OF HUMAN CAPABILITY APPLIED TO WORK

One of the most important basic human needs is to have the opportunity to use one's full capability: work is essential. Work gives individuals the opportunity to test and understand themselves in terms of their capability for making judgments and dealing with problems. When people do not have the opportunity to use their **full** capability they are dissatisfied, unmotivated and frustrated.

Until Dr. Jaques' research there was no straightforward, generally agreed upon definition of work outside the science of physics. This lack of definition has made it difficult to understand human capability as applied to human work. The requisite definition of this type of work is that it is the use of discretion and judgment in making decisions in carrying out a task. When the word 'work' is used in this book it refers to this definition of human work.

Any satisfactory measure of potential capability in work requires two things: first, a measure of level of work; and, second, a method of measuring an individual's potential to work at a given level. The measurement of level of work was described in Chapter One in terms of the longest task in a role as the measure of the complexity of a role.

Potential Capability and Applied Capability

The reason there is a particular structure in managerial hierarchies that is requisite is because of the way people use information in making decisions when they are engaged in working, that is, in problem-solving. Therefore, in order to understand these organizations, it is necessary to understand human capability and its development. There are two different aspects of human capability relevant to work in organizations. They are potential capability and applied capability.

Potential Capability

Potential Capability is the maximum level at which a person could work, given the opportunity to do so and provided s/he values the work and has the opportunity to acquire the necessary skilled knowledge. This is the level of work that people aspire to and feel satisfaction when they achieve.

It is important to understand each person's potential capability for work at any given time since that is what determines the highest level at which someone could work if he or she valued the work and had the necessary skilled knowledge. This provides a benchmark in seeking to use a given person's capability to the fullest for the good of the individual and of the organization.

Managers can and do judge each of their subordinates with regard to their current potential capability and it is one of their important accountabilities. In fact, they would not be able to keep themselves from doing so.

There are two different aspects of potential capability. The first is *Current Potential Capability* (**CPC**), which is **the highest level at which someone could work right now** if the above conditions were met. The second is *Future Potential Capability* (**FPC**), which is **the maximum level at which someone could be capable of working at some specified point in the future**, say five or ten years from now. Managers are generally able to judge both current and future potential capability with reasonable accuracy for subordinates with whom them have been working for six months or more.

For example, Jeff has a subordinate named Janice. Jeff's judgment of Janice's current potential capability is that she could currently work at his level if she had the required skilled knowledge. When considering Janice's future potential capability, he judges that she will be able to work at the next level up in the organization in about four or five years and that she most likely will be able to work one level further up toward the end of her career.

Applied Capability

Applied Capability is the capability someone has to do the work in a specific role. Applied Capability is always related to a specific role. There are three critical aspects of applied capability. First, the work must be *valued* by the person. If someone is not interested in the work s/he is doing, it is difficult to be committed to the work and to apply his or her full capability. Second, the person must have the necessary *knowledge and skills* to carry out the work or s/he will not be able to do it, no matter how much s/he wishes to do so. Finally, a person must have the *complexity of information processing* to handle the complexity of the work. Tasks, and the work required to accomplish them, vary in complexity and people vary in the complexity of information processing that they possess to apply to these tasks.

There is an important difference between the Current Potential Capability that someone has at a given time and the amount of Applied Capability the person actually uses or applies in a given task or role. Current Potential Capability is generally more than the capability that someone is applying at the present time. A person's full potential capability for work is often not reached because there is usually something out of line—the skilled knowledge may not be complete or s/he may not value that particular task sufficiently.

Values

The more a person values an activity, the more initiative s/he will take in carrying it out. The more intensely something is valued, the more strongly will it be pursued. 'Value' in this sense refers to how much individuals are committed to the role they occupy as well as the tasks and the work which make up the role. This must include not only the work content of the role, but also the value of having the role to work in.

An example of placing someone in a role she does not value occurs when an outstanding sales person is made a regional sales manager, but she does not value managing other people. She values being an outstanding salesperson, rather than being a manager and doing the work required of a manager. It will be difficult under these circumstances for her to apply her full capability to the new managerial role she has been given.

There is a proposition in requisite work that individuals do not need to be motivated or stimulated by external incentives and that people are spontaneously proactive and energetic when they do things they value, when they work for which they have the applied capability. Managers need not try to encourage output by providing incentives. Instead they need to provide conditions in which the work itself has inherent value to the people performing it. The core of what has been called motivation is actually the value someone places on something. Most people value the opportunity for work that uses their full capability.

In order for people to apply their full capability they must value the work they are doing and the role they occupy. All employees should explore their own values in the light of the work they are given to do. Managers need to be aware of and to discuss with their subordinates the kinds of work they value.

Skilled Knowledge

Knowledge is what one has learned—it can be articulated and shared. In order to work effectively in a given role, a person must have a certain background, training, education and/or experience. An engineer has to know the principles of physics and how to use them. An accountant must know accounting rules and procedures. However, it is not enough simply to have the required knowledge: it is also necessary to know how to apply the knowledge. Skill is the ability to use the knowledge one has. It is necessary to become skilled in using the knowledge that one has.

Complexity of Information Processing

A person's complexity of information processing (CIP) is the complexity of mental activity a person uses in carrying out work. CIP determines the maximum level at which that individual could work at any given time in his/her maturation and development, if s/he valued the work and had the necessary skilled knowledge. Each person's complexity of information processing is innate. The ultimate level of CIP that can be reached in one's lifetime is determined genetically, just as is one's ultimate height.

Complexity of information processing can be thought of as mental capability. It has to do with such things as:

- the number, rate of change and ease of identification of factors in a situation
- the ambiguity and complexity of factors/information that can be managed and anticipated into the future and how far into the future this can be done. This includes the ability to foresee and anticipate problems and hence to avoid or resolve them.
- the ability to pattern, order, categorize and generalize information

CIP provides the ability to do a given level of work based on its complexity. It is reflected in employees' judgment and decision making capability.

Suitability for a Role

Tasks differ in degree of difficulty: people differ in their ability to do tasks of varying complexity. The ability to do work in a specific role is based on three things, each necessary but not sufficient: complexity of information processing; knowledge, skill, experience and ability; and, values that provide the desire to do the work of the role.

Managers can judge the level of their subordinates' complexity of information processing as: at or above their own level; just right to be an immediate subordinate; or, two or more levels below their own. This last judgment provides the feeling that there is a need for one or more managers in between that subordinate and the manager making the judgment.

Managers are unable to stop themselves from making these judgments. They are a necessary part of knowing what and how to delegate to get the work of their unit done. Managers make these judgments based on experience working with their subordinates, handing off assignments and seeing the results. It takes three to six months of experience with a new subordinate to feel comfortable with judging his/her level.

Generally managers can also judge at what point in the future subordinates might be able to work at the next level up and also at what level the person may be able to work ultimately in their career.

Enabling employees to use their full capability and getting the work/tasks at the right level in the organization, staffed with individuals capable of doing the work of their role very substantially enhances productivity, profitability and employee satisfaction.

Decision Making

There is an important underlying proposition in Requisite Organization theory with regard to how people make decisions. It is that people do not make decisions through the use of knowledge that can be fully articulated prior to making those decisions. Knowledge and the skilled use of knowledge differ from decision-making. It is important to understand the distinction.

If someone can describe all the reasons why he or she is making a choice prior to doing so, that person hasn't made a decision: s/he has made a calculation. Decision making has to do with the moment of choice. People do not fully know what choice they have made until they have made it. Knowledge of all reasons for decisions and choices is always retrospective. People can only determine all reasons why they made a decision after they have made the decision. The process of choosing is at the non-verbal level and is a continuous and on-going function not only in humans but in all living organisms. Dr. Jaques discusses this concept in detail in his book entitled *The Life and Behavior of Living Organisms*. It is the complexity of this **internal** decision-making process that determines a person's potential capability.

Other Measures of Ability

None of the types of measurement presently in use, such as IQ, clinical assessments or evaluations done in assessment centers, deals with a person's ability to work at a particular level in an organization. Because the concept of human work does not have a widely understood and agreed definition and no tests have ever been validated against the ability to do work, organizations have no way to measure the differences in levels of work.

Measurement of IQ determines something quite different than that being considered in Current Potential Capability. IQ does not give any useful indication of someone's relative ability to do work in employment organizations.

Measurements done in assessment centers depend on the capability of the people on the team doing the assessing. Clinical judgments vary according to the clinical experience and ability of the person making the judgment.

With the clear and explicit definition of work—as the use of discretion and judgment in carrying out tasks—and the discovery of time-span measurement to measure differences in levels of work in roles, it has become possible to talk about actual levels of work and ability of people to carry out that work.

Personality Characteristics

Personality can be defined as the totality of traits and characteristics that are peculiar to a specific person. It has been commonly assumed that someone's basic personality characteristics are extremely important with respect to getting different kinds of work done. There are endless lists of personality traits such as being reflective, thoughtful, mature, dedicated, calm, energetic, and charismatic that are considered useful or even necessary in various aspects of work-related behavior. For example, salespeople should be gregarious, scientists should be reflective.

However, the concern in managerial systems needs to focus on whether a person is sufficiently free of pathological conditions that interfere with getting work done (which is called negative temperament in requisite work) rather than on an endless list of personality characteristics that are ambiguous and ill-defined.

The issue, for example, is not how mature a person is, but whether a person is so immature that it is difficult for that person to do his/her work. It is not how sociable someone is, but whether that person is so abrasive that it is difficult for him or her to work with others.

Negative Temperament

Temperament is defined as the method of behaving or reacting that is characteristic of a person. Where there are interpersonal stresses between individuals in the workplace and evidence of negative temperament, the first thing to look for is any organizational faults that may be making it difficult for people to work together effectively. It is only when managers are sure the organization's structure and practices are satisfactory that it is time to look at possible temperamental problems in the individuals working there.

If a negative temperamental problem (-T) is determined to exist, it is a problem to be handled by the individual, but outside the organization. It is not the organization's business to work with employees in modifying their behavior. It is, however, a manager's accountability to tell subordinates if their behavior is causing problems and the consequences of not making needed changes.

For example, Stan was a highly qualified employee who held both a doctoral degree in Physics and an MBA. He had a great deal of knowledge that was useful to the company for which he worked. However, he was extremely argumentative. He became confrontational whenever someone disagreed with his point of view. His behavior disrupted his work and the work of those around him—his manager, his subordinates and his colleagues. His manager discussed this behavior with him in terms of what was expected, but Stan, over time, did not make the desired changes. Finally, the manager determined he needed to deselect Stan from the role he was in, and he advised the MoR that Stan was too disruptive to the department to continue as his subordinate. It was subsequently arranged for Stan to leave the organization, to the relief of his co-workers.

There are many people today, experts, academics and consultants, who consider that the prime route to modifying and improving work organizations is by changing the behavior of the people involved. They attempt to do this through team building techniques, or by trying to resolve interpersonal conflicts between individuals through individual counseling, group discussions and other behavior modification methods. These attempts by an organization to change a person's behavior are counter-productive. An individual's personality or personal style is not the organization's business as long as the person performs his or her work satisfactorily and does not cause problems for other people with whom s/he interacts.

The Maturation of the Complexity of Information Processing

As was described earlier, each individual's complexity of information processing (CIP) is innate to him or her and unfolds throughout life. It is inborn. The maturation process of each person's complexity of information processing cannot be speeded up or enhanced by special educational procedures or occupational opportunities nor impeded by less favorable social, educational or occupational opportunities. These experiences are far less important for individual maturation in potential capability than are the problems that have to be solved in living everyday life. Each individual's maturation of CIP proceeds from infancy through to adulthood and on to old age. It is a natural unfolding and is predictable.

Evidence shows that individuals mature in predictable patterns and that this maturation continues throughout life, with the result being that the growth of potential can be plotted. People's ideas about 'felt fair' compensation also increase along with their growth of potential when they are in appropriate roles.

Development and Maturation

Maturation is different from development. Development refers in a general way to change through time where the eventual outcome cannot be foreseen at the beginning, such as a person's emotional development or the development of a professional practice. Maturation by contrast is predetermined and predictable.

At any given stage in a person's maturation, there is a maximum level at which that individual has the current potential capability to work. That maximum level and its rate of maturation is innate: it is genetically established just as is height. Maturation of potential capability is not affected by education or the amount of knowledge the person may acquire or by any particular experiences. An exception is that a person's maximum potential might be stunted in infancy by extreme negative factors such as severe malnutrition. Such a person as s/he matured in potential capability would appear as a damaged or handicapped higher level individual.

An individual's potential capability is an innate property of that person. By contrast, values (commitment) and knowledge can be taken up by individuals or not. Values can and do change with circumstances. Knowledge can increase, be forgotten, can be combined or can be stored for use later. A person's knowledge or values may often be confused with potential capability in the sense of someone's being judged to be ignorant or to be knowledgeable in various matters pertaining to work, or 'unmotivated' or 'highly motivated' with regard to certain work. The understanding or judgment of someone's current level of complexity of information processing is different from knowing about what work the individual values or the skilled knowledge that the person possesses.

Fairness in Employment

The idea that individuals' current and ultimate potential mental capability can be determined is a controversial proposition that seems to run counter to ideas in democratic countries of fairness and the belief that individuals ought to be able to reach any level, depending on where they want to go. In fact it is obvious to most people that some individuals have greater capability than others and greater future potential as well. Managers can readily discuss the present capability of their subordinates as well as predict with a reasonable degree of accuracy how much potential each has for handling increasingly complex work. Managers do this all the time.

The issue is not whether, in industrial societies, people should all have the opportunity to develop to whatever level they choose. It is rather that many managerial hierarchies have not found ways of ensuring that the people who work in them have the opportunity for work consistent with their potential capability. Because of the way in which most organizations are presently structured, many people do not have the opportunity to realize their full potential, with the attendant loss both to these individuals and to the organizations employing them.

Fairness in employment cannot be based on the wishful thinking that all persons can achieve any level of work they choose, but by understanding people's actual level of potential (all people, not just that of the dominant group) and ensuring that they are given the opportunity for work at their true level of potential, regardless of gender, color, age and ethnic background. Individuals, of course, must put forth the effort to acquire the necessary skilled knowledge for roles that use their potential capability.

Everyone will benefit when organizations ensure that individuals are assigned levels of work in positions that are equal to their levels of current potential capability and also ensure, as people grow in capability, that they are provided with opportunities for greater and greater levels of work, whenever this is possible. This situation not only provides fairness for the employees involved but also provides for the maximum use of capability in the company.

Complexity of Information Processing and Organization Strata

When Dr. Jaques discovered the discontinuity in organizational structure that showed up in time-span measurement, he postulated that there must be some kind of discontinuity in the way people work, a qualitative difference, that corresponded with the different strata. Through the years he found that there was indeed a difference in the way people process information when they are engaged in goal-directed behavior.

Dr. Jaques, in collaboration with Kathryn Cason, determined that there are four different ways in which people can be observed processing information, and they named these declarative, cumulative, serial and parallel. These differences are observable when people are engaged in a discussion in which they are fully engrossed.

Declarative Processing

A person using **declarative** processing explains his or her position by bringing forward a number of separate reasons for it. Each reason is stated on its own, and no connection is made with any of the other reasons that may be mentioned. For example, "Here's one of the reasons for my idea and here's another reason. I can give you several others as well". To the observer the use of information has a declarative quality and the points that are made lack unity or a sense of being connected. Each of the reasons stands alone in support of the conclusion. There is an 'or-or' quality about this type of processing. The conclusion is supported by this reason or that reason or yet another reason.

Cumulative Processing

A person using **cumulative** processing explains his or her position by bringing together a number of different ideas none of which is sufficient alone to make the case, but do so when taken together. For example, a detective might argue, "If you take this first point and put it together with this second fact and then the third clue, it becomes clear that the thief must be working inside the company." The reasons are accumulated and explicitly connected: there is a clearly stated relationship between them. This type of processing has an 'and-and' quality, that is, the position is supported by this reason and that reason and another reason.

Serial Processing

A person using **serial** processing explains his/her position by constructing a line of thought consisting of a sequence of reasons, each one of which leads on to the next, thus creating a chain of linked reasons. For example, "I think we should do A because it will lead to B and B will cause C to happen, and C will enable D to occur and that is what we want to have happen." This method of information processing has both a serial quality and a conditional quality in the sense that each reason in the series sets the conditions that lead to the next reason. That is, if this happens then that will happen which will lead to something else happening. Serial processing has an 'if-then' conditional quality—if this happens then that will happen.

Parallel Processing

A person using **parallel** processing explains his or her position by examining a number of positions, each arrived at by means of serial processing. These statements almost have the sense of the person arguing with him or herself. The several lines of thought are held in parallel and are linked to each other. Reasons or points are selected from these parallel sequences, and a new sequence is described that supports the position chosen.

An illustration of this process is, "We could do A which would then lead to B and we could get to end X. Or, we could do M, which would lead us to N, and we would arrive at another desired end, Y. Or, we could do S which would cause T and we could then achieve Z. But we might get a better outcome, W, by modifying the plan A with M and adding S. The person combines reasons or points from one or more chains to reach a desired conclusion. The nature of this, the most complex of type of information processing, is bi-conditional, meaning that only if particular consequences could be met would another series of conditions be put into place. It is the kind of processing needed to carry out critical path analysis (PERT charting) in which progress in a number of processes have to be controlled in relation to each other. There is a quality of 'if . . . then, but only if . . .' in this way of reasoning.

Orders of Complexity of Information Processing

Dr. Jaques' research has shown that there appears to be no other methods of processing information and that these four methods just described recur at higher and higher orders of complexity of information. These propositions about successively higher orders of information complexity are supported by the experience of most people in their observation that different individuals live in what almost seems to be different worlds. Six persons of differing levels of complexity of information processing placed in the same situation and faced with a common problem will perceive different sets of important features. And those six sets of information will not only differ in content, but usually also differ markedly in the amount of information obtained from observing and thinking about the situation. Each person will differ in the amount s/he is able to take into account. This is why people capable of working at high levels in an organization are commonly described as being able to handle masses of detail rapidly.

The first and second orders of information complexity belong to the world of childhood. The third and fourth orders of information complexity, called symbolic verbal and abstract conceptual, apply to the levels of work in the adult employment world from the shop or office floor to the top executives of large corporations.

Childhood Order of Information Complexity—Tangibles

In childhood the kind of information used is tangible. In early childhood the objects are concrete and in the present. There is no sense of future or past tense. This is the world of infants up to the age of about two or three. The things being discussed can be pointed to, for example, this book or that orange. A task stated at this concrete level of information complexity would be, "Take the ball". The objects are clear and unambiguous. This is the world of action. Apes and chimpanzees can operate in this world: only human beings mature into the higher levels.

The second order of complexity involves related sets of tangibles. This is the world that children mature into when they start telling stories and when they can draw stick figures. An example is, "I took the egg from the refrigerator and put it in the pan of water". Children mature from this order into the third order at varying ages from perhaps as early as 8 to 10 on into late adolescence depending on their individual rate of development.

Symbolic Verbal Order of Information Complexity

In the business world people need to be able to deal with each other without having to point to concrete examples of the things they have in mind. This order of information complexity deals with intangibles and allows work to be discussed, instructions to be issued, factories to run, new products designed, problems discussed with customers, and all the activities carried out that make it possible to manage a business unit and communicate from the shop/office floor to management levels. The variables in this order of information complexity, **symbolic verbal**, can be broken down into many concrete things and actions.

Abstract Conceptual Order of Information Complexity

From the level of the business unit president to corporations made up of many business units, or in the case of mega-corporations made up of other large corporations, ideas are used that are abstract and conceptual in nature. **Abstract conceptual** concepts are used by those with the complexity of information processing to handle the types of problems encountered at corporate levels in large corporations. Here the intangible concepts are constantly changing and exist in sets. It is the area of true strategy as against the tactics to seek to carry out the strategy. Some examples of abstract conceptual concepts are the European Union, balance sheets, treasury policies, the Pacific Rim. Embedded in each of these concepts are numbers of symbolic verbal concepts.

Universal Order of Information Complexity

This is the world of **universal** ideas and languages used in handling problems of whole societies, developing lasting philosophies or ideologies and revolutionary developments in scientific theory. The variables here are of a complexity well above those that are required for handling problems of corporate life. One of the outstanding characteristics of those few corporate leaders who develop super-corporations is that they mature into this fourth order world and take on worldwide missions. Examples of this are personal interest and participation in worldwide problems such as women's and children's health issues, AIDs, the United Nations that are taken on by corporate executives who have matured into this order of complexity.

Research in the Complexity of Information Processing

The results of extensive research on observations of these different types of complexity of information processing and orders of information complexity are described in a book co-authored by Dr. Jaques and Kathryn Cason, entitled *Human Capability*. This research demonstrates that it is possible to observe objectively and reliably the manifestation of current potential capability. The authors of *Human Capability* recommend that this type of observation be used only by managers in a requisite organization with requisite developmental and talent pool practices.

Chapter 3

WORKING RELATIONSHIPS

This chapter deals with the relationships that enable the work of the organization to get done including:

- Task Assigning Role Relationships between managers and subordinates
- Teams and Team Working
- Cross-Functional Working Relationships
- The Role of the Manager-once-Removed

All of these working relationships take place in the context of the proposition that it is a basic underlying accountability of all persons in work-related roles in a managerial hierarchy to do their best to get along with one another. This is part of the general accountability of all employees in managerial hierarchies to give their best efforts each day in their work.

THE TASK ASSIGNING ROLE RELATIONSHIP BETWEEN MANAGER AND SUBORDINATE

The essence of the manager-subordinate relationship is the delegation of tasks to be carried out. Managers make decisions about how they want the work in their unit to get done. In order for the work to be performed and the output to be achieved, managers must plan the work, set context for their subordinates and then clearly delegate the assignments.

Managerial Planning

To assign tasks appropriately, managers first have to plan how they want to get the work of their unit done. Managers cannot delegate this work to subordinates, asking them to come up with plans and planning alternatives. Managerial planning is not the work of planning departments or of subordinate planners: it is the manager's work.

In an organization that is requisitely structured, managers are able to understand the situation more fully, to plan in more comprehensive ways than their subordinate and to envisage possibilities that subordinates are not able to see. Subordinates know when their manager has the ability to do this and when s/he does not.

Subordinates can help their manager by adding details to the plans and by examining possibilities that the manager has outlined, but the final planning decisions are the manager's.

Setting Context

Delegating tasks consists of more than simply telling subordinates what to do. Managers need to communicate background information on a continuing basis, for it is this context that provides the setting in which subordinates can make informed decisions in collaboration with each other without having to come back to the manager.

Managers set context for their subordinates by providing them with the big picture within which they will be working. If the context set is too narrow, subordinates feel constrained, restricted, tightly reined in and frustrated by micro-management. This is usually the case if the manager is not one level of complexity more capable than his/her subordinates.

If the context set is too broad, subordinates feel disorganized, lost, lacking direction. They feel their manager is too distant and is someone whom they cannot understand, someone who leaves them unclear about exactly where they are going and who expects them to understand too much. This is what happens when a manager is more than one level of capability higher than the subordinate. (An exception is the case of personal assistants, who may sometimes be two levels lower in complexity than their manager, since they are in an individual contributor role that exists largely to assist with the manager's work.)

The optimum conditions for context setting are those provided by a one-step difference in complexity of information processing between manager and subordinate. Cumulative processors (those who add pieces of information to resolve a problem) can set the right context for declarative processors because they have the ability to make connections that pull together the separate, unconnected items of information used by the declarative processor. Serial processors can set context for cumulative processors by providing a chain of causal consequences within which their subordinates' cumulatively organized judgments can flow. Parallel processors can set context for serial processors because they can provide the connecting framework between multiple pathways.

The Context Trio

There are three aspects to setting full and clear context: first, managers need to let their subordinates know about the manager's goals and problems; second, they need to let subordinates know about the problems and goals of the manager's manager; and, finally, they have to keep their subordinates informed about each other's assignments. These three aspects of context can be thought of as the 'context trio'.

In setting context, managers keep subordinates informed about the managers' own goals and the objectives they are setting. Subordinates should be clear about the problems their managers have and areas in which the managers need their assistance in order to get various tasks and project work completed. Managers should inform their subordinates about these same issues with regard to the manager's manager, providing the larger picture. From time to time, managers should provide this information in a three-level meeting that includes both their immediate subordinates and the subordinates' subordinates. (In requisite work subordinates' subordinates are referred to as Subordinates-once-Removed or SoRs.)

Managers also provide information so that their subordinates understand each other's assignments, enabling them to work knowledgeably together. Having information about each other's relevant tasks helps subordinates work together as an effective managerial team. Setting regular and sufficient context saves a great deal of time both for managers and subordinates.

Task, Work and Role

Specific definitions of work, role and task were introduced in Chapter One. They are reviewed here because these concepts underlie effective delegation of tasks. A task is an assignment to produce a specific output. The words task and assignment are used interchangeably. Work is what a person has to do to carry out a task: it is the construction of a pathway to achieve the output and the use of judgment to overcome obstacles encountered en route to the completion of that output. A role is a position in the organization where tasks are aggregated and an individual is placed to carry out those tasks.

Specifying Tasks

As was discussed in Chapter One, when delegating a task a manager must specify or ensure that the following are understood by the subordinate: quantity (Q), quality (Q), time by when the task is to be completed (T), available resources (R), and relevant policies or procedures. Tasks can be thought of as a 'what by when'. Managers often neglect to explicitly state by when they need a task or assignment completed, yet they do have a maximum time in mind since they must coordinate and integrate all the assignments of their unit. A useful reminder for managers when delegating tasks is to specify clearly each aspect of QQT/R (Quantity, Quality, Target Completion Time and available Resources).

Outputs have Value

When managers set tasks for their subordinates they are transmitting their own values: they are indicating that they value the results of the work they have assigned. What is required of subordinates is that they accept their manager's valuing of the assigned task, even if the subordinate does not value the task or the results of the assigned work. The expectation is that employees will treat the work they have been given to do with the same value that is placed on that work by the manager and by the organization. This is not the same as a subordinate valuing a role as a whole. All roles usually contain tasks that one would rather not do but are part of the role and must be completed.

How Far Down to Delegate

The art of delegation is to understand the nature of the work needed to complete a given task and then to delegate that work to the right level in the organization. Work should not be delegated to too low a level. Delegating tasks to too low a level is costly—the work takes longer, more resources are used than necessary and the quality is lower, if the tasks get completed at all.

In a recurring fad sometimes referred to as 'empowerment', the idea is to push work as far down in the organization as possible. True empowerment consists of delegating work to the correct level, thus providing people with challenging work that they are capable of doing in their own way. Delegating a task to the right level with an appropriate amount of resources results in the task being completed at the desired time, in the desired quantity and of the right quality, by a satisfied employee.

Manager's Integration of the Unit's Functions

Managers do not delegate all of their functions and processes. They can delegate part of their work into subordinate roles in the tasks they assign, but they must add value to each of them. The manager adds value by setting sufficient context and by solving problems the subordinate cannot solve. The weaving together of the work and functions of the unit remains with the manager as well. It is the manager's accountability to integrate the work of the unit.

For example, a business unit head can delegate production, marketing and selling functions but retains the accountability for adding value by providing the over-arching context and the decisions that weld all of the functions together.

Types of Delegated Tasks

Managers get work done in three ways. They do it themselves, they get help from subordinates or they delegate the task completely to a subordinate. Thus, there are two different types of delegated tasks. The distinction between them is useful to both managers and subordinates. Managers can delegate a task as a direct output of the person to whom the task has been assigned or the manager can delegate a task that is part of the manager's work and is given back to the manager.

Direct Output

Direct Output (DO) is a tangible or intangible finished product or service that will be sent out to someone (either within the organization or outside it). When a service or product is handed off, it becomes direct output. The person who has been delegated the direct output decides when the finished output is good enough to send out. The finished product or service does not have to be reviewed or approved by that person's manager. First-line work is largely direct output. Direct output can, however, come out of the managerial hierarchy at any level. Managers can produce direct output themselves rather than delegate certain tasks to subordinates.

Delegated Direct Output

Managers delegate tasks to their subordinates. This is **Delegated Direct Output** (DDO). Some of the tasks a manager assigns to subordinates can be delegated further down through the organization to whatever level is appropriate to have the work completed. When managers delegate tasks to subordinates, part of their planning is to think about the level at which the work needs to be completed and to specify when they do not want the work to be delegated further down.

For example, a vice president of human resources wants a workshop to be prepared on interviewing techniques. She decides to delegate the task to the director of management development with specific instructions that the director is to prepare the material himself and not delegate the design of the workshop to a subordinate trainer.

Direct Output Support and Aided Direct Output

Both managers and subordinates have direct output work. Managers do not delegate all of their tasks to their subordinates: managers have some work they must do themselves. When managers are the ones to complete a task, they often need help in doing so and need to get direct output support.

When a subordinate provides the manager with **Direct Output Support** (DOS), the manager is producing **Aided Direct Output** (ADO). These two ideas always go together; that is, any time someone is receiving direct output support (DOS) that person is in the process of producing aided direct output (ADO).

This occurs, for example, when the unit manager who is accountable to complete the annual departmental budget asks first-line managers in the unit for budget estimates for their sections. These go to the unit manager who is producing the unit budget and the manager is producing aided direct output. The first-line managers are doing direct output support work.

When assigning tasks, clarity is enhanced when the manager specifies that the subordinate is assisting with manager's work by providing Direct Output Support or, where the task is Delegated Direct Output, that the task is delegated to the subordinate to complete.

Individual Contributors and ADO/DOS

The individual contributor role was described in Chapter One as anyone who is mainly engaged in producing direct outputs and is the person who signs off on these outputs. An individual contributor does not delegate his/her work but may get some of it done as aided direct output through subordinates who provide direct output support. If individual contributors need help in getting their work done and are provided with people to help them, they then become managers of those individuals. Most of the work of these subordinates goes back to the individual contributor.

A chief scientist, for example, doing her own research work and sending the result of that work out is doing direct output work as an individual contributor. This person has subordinates to assist her in doing parts of the work, helping her to produce the output. She is the manager of these people, but she is the one who completes the work, determines its quality and decides when it is ready to be released.

Another example is the case of a project engineer who produces designs for the manufacturing department. The engineer has subordinate technicians to help her work on detailed portions of the design. The work of the subordinates goes back to the project engineer who integrates it into her work and it becomes part of the engineer's final product. The engineer is doing ADO work and the technicians have DOS tasks.

TEAMS AND TEAM WORKING

A 'team' in requisite work can be defined as a group of people who work together to achieve a specific output for which there is an accountable manager. Teams and team working are essential for any organization to work effectively across functions.

There are three types of teams in requisite organization: project, coordinative and managerial. Project teams have an accountable manager for whom they produce an output. This, like the manager-subordinate relationship, is a task-assigning relationship. Coordinative teams consist of a number of people representing different functions whose work needs to be synchronized. The third type consists of a manager's subordinates, who can be thought of as a managerial team.

Project Teams

All requisite project teams, sometimes called ad hoc teams or task forces, should have a manager for whom the work is carried out and who is accountable for the output of the team. These teams are resources that managers use to help them solve problems or accomplish tasks.

The accountable manager specifies the tasks with regard to the target completion time and the quantity and quality desired and also secures and provides resources for the team. Project teams may be made up of people chosen from a manager's own unit, or people selected from across several units when cross-functional expertise is needed. The manager accountable for the project team may or may not appoint a team leader. When the work of the project team is completed the team is disbanded.

Project Team Leaders

The accountable manager may choose to assign a project team leader rather than head the work of the team directly. When this is the case the person appointed has the same task assigning role relationships and managerial authority as the manager except for that of appraising the effectiveness of team members. Project team leaders can:

- veto the appointment of a person to the team s/he considers unsuitable
- request removal of a team member judged not capable of the required work
- call meetings
- assign tasks to team members
- coordinate and integrate the work of the team

Project team leaders are accountable for the output of the team and for getting the collaboration and confidence of their team members. The team leader discusses with the immediate manager of each team member that person's effectiveness as a member of the team. The immediate manager carries out the appraisal.

Project Team Members

Individuals are requested to participate on a team by the team's accountable manager. An estimate of the time required is provided since the individual's manager may need to modify some of that person's task assignments. By agreeing to make any given subordinate available for work on a team, the immediate manager of that person demonstrates that s/he values the work of the team.

If subordinates find that the time needed for the work of a team they are on is interfering with their ability to get the work done on their usual assigned tasks, they discuss this with their immediate manager and resolve the issue.

Team members are to bring their full capability to bear on the work of the team. They are to attempt to resolve any team and departmental conflicts with the team, the team leader and the team's accountable manager. Any conflicts that cannot be resolved are to be referred to the team member's immediate manager who then discusses it with the team's accountable manager.

Project Team Output

Teams are often formed to provide direct output support (DOS) to the accountable manager who has decided s/he needs the help of several people who may be within his or her own unit, or from across several units. It is also possible for the accountable manager to delegate direct output to a team. If this is done, the accountable manager must appoint a project team leader so that there is a person accountable for the team's direct output.

Individual contributors may also need a team to provide them with direct output support. The individual contributor then becomes the manager accountable for the output of any team that s/he forms. An individual contributor would not delegate direct output to a team. Output of individual contributors is their own.

Coordinative Teams

Project teams differ from coordinative teams because the coordinative team leader does not have task-assigning authority. Coordinative teams are used in situations where the work of a group of people representing a number of functions must be coordinated over a period of time. This type of team is described later in this chapter in the section on cross-functional working relationships.

Managerial Teams

Because the use of the concept of a 'team' is so pervasive in organizations, a manager's subordinates can be thought of as a manager's team. They are permanently part of the manager's team by virtue of the role they occupy. There are several types of managerial teams including:

- all of a manager's immediate subordinates
- three stratum teams made up of immediate subordinates and subordinates-once-removed
- all of a manager's subordinates at all levels

No Team Decisions

In working together as a team, subordinates are actively encouraged to express dissent, to explore pros and cons and to engage in debate with the manager or project team leader and with each other. But, when there are decisions to be made, the accountable manager or the accountable project leader makes them.

In a managerial hierarchy, decisions are made by individuals. People are employed as individuals, not as groups, and are held accountable for decisions as individuals. There are no group decisions and no self-managed teams in a requisite organization.

CROSS-FUNCTIONAL WORKING RELATIONSHIPS

Managerial organizations need an extensive network of relationships between persons who cannot directly assign tasks to each other. These are people in roles who are immediate subordinates of the same manager or who are subordinates of different managers. The designation of cross-functional working relationships describes the exact nature of the relationship and clarifies the authority and accountability of each role involved with respect to certain specified activities or situations.

Cross-Functional Relationships Exist Between Roles

Cross-Functional Working Relationships (CFWRs) are established between roles, not between people. Frequently, what has seemed to be a clash of personalities disappears when working relationships are clearly spelled out. Employees know where they stand with each other, they know who is accountable for doing what and who has the authority to do what in relation to other roles. Establishing these relationships between roles enables disagreements and problem resolution, often caused by insufficient resources, to move up in the organization to a level where the issue can be resolved. For example, the task may need to be changed or more resources may need to be provided.

Establishing Cross-Functional Working Relationships

The Manager-once-Removed establishes CFWRs as a means of integrating the work of the organization across functional areas. Immediate managers, and often the individuals currently filling the roles, are consulted and can suggest which CFWR might be most effective in a given situation, but it is the MoR who makes the decision.

Where the relationship needs to be specified between roles at different levels in the organization, the type of CFWR is decided by the first cross-over manager. A cross-over manager is the first common manager of the roles involved. The MoR or cross-over manager communicates decisions about cross-functional accountability and authority to the individuals concerned and their immediate managers.

Designated cross-functional working relationships can be expected to change as conditions change and as the work in roles change. They need to be reviewed from time to time to determine if different CFWRs are needed.

Exploring CFWRs

If the person in a cross-functional working relationship who needs to initiate a task or take an action is designated as person A and the person who must respond is designated as B, here are some of the questions that arise in thinking about and determining what kind of accountability and authority to assign to integrate work:

Can A advise B?

Can A try to persuade B about something?

Can A tell B to delay doing something?

Can A tell B to stop doing something?

Can A tell B what to do?

Does A need a service from B in order to complete an assignment?

Does A need to get Bs to work together toward a common goal?

Can A report higher in the organization if B does not cooperate?

The Seven Cross-Functional Working Relationships

There are seven different cross-functional working relationships. The first is the Collateral Relationship and is the only one that exists between all immediate subordinates of a given manager. The other six CFWRs exist between roles at one or more remove from the cross-over manager. These are called Advisory, Monitoring Auditing, Prescribing, Service and Coordinative. These six relationships exist between persons who are subordinates of different managers.

Four of the CFWRs are related in nature and carry an increasing amount of accountability and authority. These are Advisory, Monitoring, Auditing and Prescribing. The remaining two CFWRs are called Service and Coordinative. Service accountability and authority is the most common CFWR. Coordinative accountability and authority is used when it is necessary for someone to integrate the work of a number of other persons.

Brief descriptions of the seven CFWRs are given below. Because these relationships are so critical to integrating work across functions, more detailed descriptions of each are also provided along with an example.

Collateral Relationship

The Collateral Relationship is the foundation of effective cross-functional working. Colleague subordinates of the same manager frequently have work that impinges on each other's, yet they are not accountable for each other's work. In this relationship each of the subordinates has the accountability and the authority to try to persuade the other regarding their respective needs. In the collateral relationship people cannot tell each other what to do, but their common manager can expect them to work things out in a satisfactory way. They are not to fight about who is right. If they cannot agree they then attempt to resolve the issue as they believe their manager would want the situation handled. If they cannot come to a mutually agreeable solution that they think would be satisfactory to their manager, then they go **together** to see him/her.

Advisory Relationship

Persons who have advisory accountability and authority are held accountable by their managers for providing information to designated individuals. The advisees are required, by their own managers, to keep the advisor informed about their work and to listen to the advisor's advice. Individuals whose roles have advisory accountability and authority are not held accountable as to whether or not the persons being advised act on their advice. It is the accountability of each individual's manager to see that the advice is used appropriately.

Monitoring Relationship

In a Monitoring Relationship, the monitor has the accountability and authority to be kept informed about the relevant activities of the person being monitored. A, the monitor, can try to persuade B to change what s/he is doing if A is not satisfied with what is happening in the area that s/he has the accountability to monitor. If A is still not satisfied, A can ask B to delay taking action. A then takes the matter up with his/her manager, who decides with B's manager what is to be done. The matter is resolved between the respective managers, and B's manager tells B what s/he should do. Taking the matter up higher is part of A's accountability and authority. If A does not do so, it is assumed A is satisfied with what B is doing.

Auditing Relationship

Auditing accountability and authority usually occurs only when there is some kind of threat to the organization, perhaps with regard to safety, environmental or financial issues. It is not enough, for example, for the persons with accountability in areas such as legal and regulatory merely to be able to try to persuade others to do something in critical areas. In addition to being informed about their work, the auditor is also accountable for requiring designated persons to stop doing something that s/he judges to be out of line with prescribed boundaries and where serious consequences may result. If they disagree, the matter is taken up to their respective managers.

Prescribing Relationship

This is the strongest lateral working relationship and is only used when health and safety issues are at stake. It is sometimes necessary for person A not only to tell person B to stop doing something but also for A to tell B to take a different kind of action if necessary, in order to avert a serious outcome or disaster. This is called prescribing accountability and authority and usually is held by someone who is an expert in a particular field or discipline.

Service Relationship

There are always two parts to the service relationship, the service-getter and the service-giver. They are authorized, respectively, to request and to provide the service in question. If the service-giver cannot provide the needed service for whatever reason, the service-getter must take the matter higher to his or her own manager. This generally happens when there is a shortage of resources that must be resolved by the relevant managers.

Coordinative Relationship

With coordinative accountability and authority A, the coordinator, has the authority to bring together the people whose work s/he is coordinating and to try to persuade them to take a suitable course of action. Coordinative accountability and authority is used where there is a group of people who need to be coordinated in some kind of action or process and need to be called together from time to time. This accountability and authority is given to leaders of coordinative teams.

Collateral Accountability and Authority

Collateral accountability and authority occur in the work of two or more immediate subordinates of the same manager, and who must interact in a manner of mutual accommodation. As has already been mentioned, **collateral is the only cross-functional working relationship between immediate subordinates of the same manager**. The obligation of immediate subordinates to work together brings about critical integration of the work within each manager's area, starting with the subordinates of the chief executive officer.

Each of the colleagues in a collateral relationship has the accountability and authority to:

- try to persuade his/her colleague to take appropriate action that could facilitate the task with which they are involved and increase its effectiveness
- solve problems based on the context set by the manager
- accommodate the other's needs as far as possible
- refer to their mutual manager any significant problems that cannot be resolved

All immediate subordinates of a manager have collateral accountability and authority with regard to each other and cooperative collateral relationships are required.

Example

The president is the common manager of the vice president of sales and the vice president of production in a business unit. The sales vice president has the authority to try to persuade the production vice president to produce more, even though the production unit is up to capacity and scheduling this additional production will drive up costs because of overtime. The president has to be able to rely on these two colleagues to try to find a solution they know she would want them to have. It may satisfy neither of them, or it may satisfy one and not the other, but the president can expect them to work things out in a way that will be satisfactory to her. They can neither tell each other what to do nor stop each other from taking any particular action, but they can try to persuade each other. Only if they cannot come to the kind of solution that they think would be satisfactory to the president do they go together to discuss the situation with her.

Advisory Accountability and Authority

In the advisory relationship the person giving the advice (the advisor or expert) has the accountability and authority to:

- take the initiative in approaching the advisee and presenting ideas or information that may be useful
- take the time to explain to the advisee where and why the ideas may be useful
- be kept informed about the activities and problems of the advisee

There are clear limitations to an advisor's accountability and authority as follows:

- if the advisee does not accept the expert's advice, then the matter must rest there as far as the advisor is concerned. The expert will proceed no further.

- the advisor must not report the advisee's reaction to his/her advice to any other person. It is for the advisees' managers to judge how effectively subordinates are using advisory resources.

If an expert needs to have stronger authority than this, the advisor should instead be given monitoring accountability and authority. In the monitoring relationship the monitor can instruct the person in the role being monitored to delay an action until the matter is brought to a higher level in the organization.

Advisory accountability and authority is a way to ensure that the best use is made of resident experts. With their advisory role relationship clearly spelled out, experts are able to take the initiative in offering their expertise in the form of unsolicited advice to specified others. However, it is essential to define precisely who is authorized to take the initiative to give advice to whom and about what.

In addition, subordinates have advisory accountability and authority in relation to their own managers. If a subordinate thinks of something that might be important to his or her own work or to the manager's work, the subordinate is accountable for advising the manager.

Example

The corporate CEO gives the corporate economist advisory accountability and authority to meet with each of the organization's business unit presidents to give them advice when there are major economic issues as well as information about what she thinks they ought to take into account when doing their work. The economist has the authority to go to see the specified individuals to provide them with information and they have to listen. However, it is the accountability of their manager, the corporate EVP, to ensure that each BU president notes the advice and uses that information appropriately.

Monitoring Accountability and Authority

Monitoring accountability and authority is needed in situations in which it is necessary to ensure that employees are adhering to policies and maintaining adequate standards by subjecting what they are doing to critical review. Examples of this are financial limits, technical standards and interpretation of policy.

A person operating in the monitoring capacity has the authority to:

- be informed about the activities and issues of the people being monitored
- discuss possible improvements with them and/or their managers
- try to persuade them to modify their present practices and procedures where necessary and, if not satisfied, to get them to delay until the matter is referred to the relevant managers
- recommend new policies or standards where required
- report sustained or significant deficiencies to his or her own manager

The monitoring component does *not* give authority to:

- permanently stop people from doing something
- instruct people to change their present practices and procedures
- judge the personal effectiveness of the person being monitored and report on him/her personally
- set new policies and standards

Monitoring involves persuasion but, unlike the advising role, the matter can be taken higher when the monitor is not satisfied with the results of the persuasion. If there is disagreement and the monitor chooses not to exercise his/her authority, then it means the monitor does not consider the disagreement to be serious and is prepared to accept accountability for letting the matter rest.

Example

A development specialist has perfected a chemical cleaning process and has been given monitoring accountability and authority for ensuring that it is used effectively in a given unit. The specialist has the authority and accountability to go to the appropriate first-line managers in the unit, to stay informed about how the use of the new process is proceeding and to decide if the cleaning work is taking place in a satisfactory way. If the specialist is not satisfied he can try to persuade the person controlling the new cleaning process to make the necessary modifications.

The person being monitored may say, for example, "Look, this is too costly, I really can't do it this new way. This is the best I can do." If the specialist is not satisfied, he is accountable for taking the matter to his manager to see if there is some way to use the procedure properly. The person being monitored knows that this is what the specialist must do.

Auditing Accountability and Authority

Auditing accountability and authority is used to maintain the quality of the organization's processes and products.

A person in an auditing role has the authority to:

- have access to the work of specified others
- inspect the work in accordance with corporate procedures
- stop someone from doing something that is outside acceptable limits

If the auditor decides that the work being inspected is outside the rules, regulations, policies, tolerances or other limits governing it, the auditor has the authority to instruct the other person to stop doing the work unless and until it can be brought within the organization's agreed standards.

The auditor/inspector does not have the authority to:

- instruct the other person on what to do (if that is necessary then the accountability and authority must be that of prescribing)
- judge the effectiveness of the person being audited and report on him or her personally

If the person whose task is being audited disagrees, he or she must nevertheless stop and then refer the issue to his/her own manager.

Auditing accountability and authority has more force than that of monitoring. It is used for situations that might develop into an emergency or to deal with critical issues such as an environmental, legal or financial threat or where someone is operating too near the margin of safety in a situation or is just over that margin.

Example

A boiler operator has set the boiler pressures so close to the margin of safety that the safety officer believes the boiler may explode. The safety officer has been given auditing accountability and authority for these situations. In addition to having the authority to try to persuade the boiler operator to make modifications in the pressure he uses, the safety officer can also tell him to stop operating in the way she believes to be unsafe, until they have both discussed the matter with their managers and the managers have discussed the situation with each other.

Prescribing Accountability and Authority

Prescribing accountability and authority is the strongest of all cross-functional accountability and authority. Here person A can require person B to do something and B must do it. B can raise questions afterwards if s/he is dissatisfied with A's prescription. When there is a difference of opinion between A and B and A has prescribing authority, then A makes the decision. B must do as A instructs.

Wherever there is danger that a catastrophe could result either from failure to conform to established limits or from interpretation of those limits, or in the event of an emergency situation, it is necessary to provide experts to make external checks on the work being done and for these experts to have prescribing accountability and authority.

Example

In an organization that moves a dangerous chemical by truck throughout the country one role has been designated prescribing accountability and authority in the event of an emergency. If a road accident occurs the individual in this role is notified and all persons working for the company must do exactly as he instructs until the emergency situation is under control.

Service Accountability and Authority

Service-getting and service-giving accountability and authority are the most widespread cross-functional working relationships in most organizations. Clearly establishing the service component of relationships so that services are provided smoothly substantially increases work and organizational effectiveness. This requires that everyone is clear about the specific services they can get and the services they must give, and about how to act appropriately if they are unable to get or to give the authorized services. Service-getters need to have clearly specified what services they are authorized to get, and from whom, and service-givers need to know what services they must provide and to whom.

The service-giver cannot decide that s/he will not give an authorized service but must have the authority to decide when s/he cannot do so by the time requested. For example, s/he may not have the necessary resources to provide the service. When a service-giver cannot provide the service within the time requested by the service-getter, s/he must report the difficulty to his/her manager, who then resolves the problem and negotiates any delays or reduction of service with the manager of the service-getter.

The service-getter who is confronted by sustained difficulty getting the service required in a timely fashion is accountable for taking the matter to his/her own manager. The service-getter's manager then has the opportunity to negotiate an improved and consistent service provision with the manager of the service-giver.

When the limits of service-giving and service-getting are clearly spelled out and understood by all parties, wasteful and costly service and interpersonal difficulties can usually be avoided.

Example

A first-line manager (FLM) is authorized by her manager to get services from the maintenance technician. The technician has the accountability and authority to provide maintenance services to specified first-line managers. The maintenance technician does not have the authority to tell the FLM he cannot provide the service. He does have the authority to tell the FLM he cannot provide it right away and to tell her by when it can be done. The FLM may not try to persuade the technician do it by when she needs the work completed. If she is unsuccessful in getting the service she requires in a timely fashion, she refers the matter to her manager, who discusses it with the manager of the technician.

The FLM is not reporting about 'bad' service, but is taking the matter higher in an effort to postpone the maintenance until the technician can do it, to get more resources allocated to maintenance or to be given the authority to seek maintenance services elsewhere. The matter is referred up a level to where the problem can be resolved.

Coordinative Accountability and Authority

Coordinative accountability and authority is useful as a means of arranging for a number of people to work together who are not subordinate to the same manager. The function of the coordinator is to persuade a group or team of people from different functions to work together in a joint undertaking. The coordinator and the individuals whose efforts are to be coordinated are specified by their own managers.

The coordinator has the accountability and authority to:

- propose how tasks should be approached
- keep the group informed of progress in carrying out the tasks
- help overcome setbacks and problems encountered

In order to carry out these functions, the coordinator has the authority to:

- try to persuade the others to act together to implement plans for action
- arrange meetings
- obtain necessary information from team members
- take issues and disagreements to his/her manager if persuasive efforts fail to settle the problem

A coordinator does not have the authority to issue overriding instructions when there are disagreements. If a coordinative team member is not participating as fully as needed, the leader/coordinator reports the problem to his/her manager, who takes up the issue with the manager of that function. The manager with functional accountability for the issues resolves any problems that the coordinator in unable to resolve.

Example

New sales territories have been laid out and some national accounts have been identified. The shifting of accounts has to be done in a smooth fashion. One regional manager is assigned coordinative accountability and authority in regard to implementing these changes. This regional manager will get all of the sales representatives involved together and persuade them to time their actions in a coordinated fashion, and will help coordinate the common courses of action that seem best for the customers and the company.

Summary of Cross-Functional Working Relationships

In these role relationships the person with the specified accountability and authority is not held accountable for what the other person does except in the cases of auditing and prescribing. Person A, with the designated accountability and authority. can initiate activity but the other person, B, has the authority to decide whether or not to accept the instruction or initiation. The manager of A, the initiator, is accountable for the A's work in relation to the other person, B. B's manager is accountable for B's work and outputs.

In the case of prescribing and auditing accountability and authority, the auditor can tell person B to stop doing something and the prescriber can tell B what to do, or what action to take to avert some kind of serious event. The instructions to delay or to do something must be carried out by B, who can refer questions to his/her own manager afterwards. Prescribing and auditing accountability and authority are generally specified only for serious circumstances. Ordinarily one would want to provide coordinative or monitoring accountability and authority, or even, where appropriate, the lesser advisory type of accountability and authority.

THE ROLE OF THE MANAGER-ONCE-REMOVED

Dr. Jaques identified the significant relationship between managers and the subordinates of their subordinates. The managers in this relationship are referred to as Managers-once-Removed (MoRs) and the subordinates' subordinates are referred to as Subordinates-once-Removed (SoRs). This three-level relationship is essential for effective resource allocation, communication, individual development and fairness. Specific aspects of the MoR's accountability and authority with regard to SoRs are described in the remainder of this chapter.

Assign SoR Roles

Managers-once-Removed decide *how many* subordinate roles at the SoR level there will be and at *what level* within the stratum these roles are positioned, because these are major resourcing decisions. MoRs do not leave it to their immediate subordinates to decide how many subordinate roles they shall have and where those roles will be positioned. Immediate managers have the authority to decide *what tasks* they assign to their subordinates' roles.

Decide SoR Cross-Functional Working Relationships

As described above, the MoR has the authority to make the final decision on cross-functional working relationships in order to integrate the work flow across functional areas.

Talent Pool Development and Succession Planning

To compete successfully in the marketplace it is necessary to ensure that an organization has a sufficient number of available, trained, and capable people to do both current work and anticipated future work. Immediate managers deal with their subordinates' ongoing work, evaluate how effectively they are performing in their role and coach them so that they can fill their roles more effectively, but it is the Manager-once-Removed who looks at all of his or her SoRs to see who has the potential capability to move up, when and if opportunities are available.

There has been a widespread belief that every good manager ought to select his or her successor. This procedure has serious problems. What if an MoR's subordinate selects a successor who is not satisfactory to the MoR as an immediate subordinate or the MoR does not believe that person is capable of working at that level. Managers are not required to have as a subordinate someone they do not believe can do the work the role requires. MoRs have accountability and the authority for evaluating their SoRs' current and future potential and for judging promotability.

Individual Development

In a requisite organization Managers-once-Removed are accountable for establishing development plans for their Subordinates-once-Removed. MoRs are the persons who are most directly concerned with the talent pool and the long-range development of their SoRs.

In a process Dr. Jaques called mentoring, MoRs work with each SoR individually with regard to that person's work future and career development, training and education, beyond that needed in his/her present role. SoRs discuss their aspirations and career opportunities in the company with their MoRs, not with their immediate managers. Immediate managers are concerned with their subordinates' continuing growth and development in their current role.

Transfer Decisions

MoRs determine when they want individual SoRs transferred as, perhaps, part of their career development or to fill a role that has become vacant. The MoR discusses this with the SoR's immediate manager before making a decision. An immediate manager can also recommend a transfer when s/he sees the person might be suitable for a particular role, but the MoR makes the decision.

Deselection and Dismissal with Cause

When a manager finds that a subordinate is not able to do the work of the role, the MoR works with Human Resources to try to find the person an appropriate role within the organization. The MoR determines the issue of separation from company employment of a Subordinate-once-Removed if it should become necessary.

If an immediate manager finds it necessary to recommend the dismissal of an immediate subordinate for serious negligence or some flagrant breaking of rules and regulations, the MoR has the accountability for seeing that the dismissal decision follows the proper legal procedures and is within policy. With regard to these difficult people issues, an MoR needs to ensure that, in his or her judgment, procedures are being handled fairly.

Provision for Appeal

SoRs have the authority and must have the opportunity to tell their MoR when they want to appeal their immediate manager's judgment because they feel they are being unfairly treated. An example would be an SoR who believes he is being more harshly treated than some of his colleagues. This opportunity for appeal is an important condition that gives people a sense of fairness and justice.

Equilibration

Managers-once-Removed are also accountable for ensuring even treatment of their SoRs by their immediate managers. In requisite work this is called equilibration. MoRs judge whether or not their SoRs are getting reasonably equitable treatment from their managers, and MoRs have discussions with their immediate subordinate managers in this regard as necessary.

Ensure Effective Managerial Leadership

MoRs are accountable for using management practices and for ensuring that their immediate subordinate managers use them as well. MoRs work with and observe the way in which their immediate subordinate managers are handling their subordinates, the manager's SoRs, both as individuals and in team working so that they have a good sense of their effectiveness in managerial leadership work.

Three-Level Managerial Team Working

As was mentioned earlier, from time to time MoRs hold meetings between their individual immediate subordinates and their SoRs. When the three levels are all together, the MoR can give the group a sense of where the business is going, discuss corporate policies, and review problem areas. These meetings allow MoRs to observe their SoRs at work, observations that are necessary for the MoR's career development and mentoring accountabilities. These three-level meetings also provide an opportunity for people to get to know each other and an atmosphere that strengthens collaborative effort and facilitates the cooperativeness of employees with each other.

Chapter 4

ORGANIZATION STRUCTURE & FUNCTIONAL ALIGNMENT

There are certain functions that can be generalized for all managerial hierarchies. This chapter examines the major functions that are necessary at given levels of organizations, providing a framework for how work should be organized and roles should be established.

FUNCTIONS IN AN ORGANIZATION

Function refers to a particular type of work or cluster of activities that is required by the objectives of an organization. Functions are particular kinds of work, for example, marketing, manufacturing or providing services such as legal or accounting to other parts of the organization. The 'alignment' of functions refers to the process of grouping functions to provide the best fit in a role or in a department.

The first step in aligning functions and establishing a requisite structure is the articulation of the organization's vision and mission by the owners or board of directors. Based on this, the CEO provides direct personal leadership in deciding the corporate goals and objectives and the strategy for achieving them.

Determining corporate strategy includes deciding what functions are needed and at what level of complexity the work needs to be done, hence the stratum in which the functions should be placed. For example, if corporate research and development work has a 15-year perspective, the work needs to be done in a role at Stratum VI. However, if the work only needs an eight-year time frame, it can be established in a role at Stratum V.

Strategic planning includes determining which functions the organization needs, aligning functions in an effective manner, and establishing those functions in the right stratum, based on the level of work the CEO determines is required to carry out the function. This strategy is the basis for establishing a requisite organization structure for the aligned functions.

An organization structure that is requisite is a system of role relationships. The essential functions in those roles enable the organization to operate as required by the nature of the work to be done and the nature of the human beings involved.

Business Units

In corporations that contain multiple business units there are two main groupings of functions, those that are corporate and those belonging to the individual business unit. The first grouping, functions needed at the corporate level, includes operations, corporate development work and corporate services. The second group of functions are those of the smaller, typically Stratum V, business units within the corporation. These include the six mainstream business functions of production, marketing, selling, procurement, delivery and product development/enhancement as well as the three supporting functions: services, resource sustainment and resource enhancement.

Stratum V business units within the large Stratum VII corporation generally appears to be the most effective way of structuring. This may be related to how far into the future finite planning can be carried out. It appears that about seven years forward is the longest period over which people are capable of planning and carrying out finitely budgeted projects and that this period is the longest outreach for systematic predicting and forecasting. Beyond ten years a conceptual approach is needed in which the future is constructed rather than forecasted. This phenomenon may underlie the fact that Stratum V business units with a five to ten year time-span seems to be the ideal level to establish a single unified whole business system.

However, sometimes the time frame of what has to be done in Stratum VII corporations makes it necessary to do the work in business units established at Stratum IV or VI. The same functions are required in these business units.

Some businesses need to be conducted in one large Stratum V or Stratum VI business unit because of the nature of the product or the market place, such as oil refining or automobile production. (In these instances it becomes even more critical to establish very clear cross-functional working relationships and coordinative teams.) The existence of a single corporate business unit does not eliminate the need for the Stratum VII corporate functions necessary to maintain a national/global perspective on social, political, economic, values and technological changes that are occurring. The CEO should also continually seek the opportunity to devolve the single large business unit into small Stratum V business units, if possible.

When a business unit operation is stand-alone and not part of a larger corporation, the most complex work of the company may be at Stratum IV, III or even II, rather than at Stratum V. This will be explored in more detail later in this chapter.

STRATUM VII CORPORATIONS

A Stratum VII corporation generally requires a number of functions whose purpose is to oversee the work of groups of business units and to enhance their asset value while maintaining a profitable balance sheet for the business as a whole. The Stratum VII CEO must do the strategic work necessary to enable the Stratum V business units to operate successfully and at the same time must ensure the future business development of the corporation by finding or internally developing new business opportunities and adding and divesting business units as necessary.

The CEO must develop the organization's competitive strategy, keep the consequences of that strategy under review and must network nationally and internationally to keep strategy in line with worldwide developments. The CEO must give his/her own direct personal leadership to the process of deciding the corporate strategic thrust.

Other functions of the CEO include ensuring that the business is financially strong, has essential information, planning and control systems and has the necessary human resources throughout the corporation both for the current needs and to staff the constantly evolving organization.

The corporation's Stratum VI roles are established to help the CEO carry out his/her work in performing the functions just described. The number of Stratum VI roles that are necessary is a matter of the CEO's judgment. These Stratum VI corporate roles may have subordinates in Stratum V and IV depending upon the requirements of the work.

Corporate Operations Vice Presidents

To the extent that there are groupings of business units, one or more corporate operations executive vice president roles are required at Stratum VI, each with a portfolio of business units. These corporate executive vice presidents operate in a ten- to fifteen-year thrust, setting context for their business units that are typically operating in five- to seven-year thrusts. The corporate executive vice presidents are accountable for the financial results of each of their subordinate business unit presidents.

How business units are grouped is a matter of corporate strategy, determined by the requirements of the marketplace. Strategic groupings of business units are temporary in nature and can be altered in response to changing business circumstances. Business units may be grouped for reasons of common markets, common geography, common production or common products.

The Stratum VI operational executive vice presidents should not require many support staff roles. They may need a small personal staff, but the emphasis is on the executive vice presidents doing their own work, both within the organization and in the outside world, of adding value to the work of the business units by sustaining conditions in which they can function effectively and by developing the Stratum V and IV corporate talent pool.

Corporate Development Officers

Corporate development work is concerned with keeping abreast of technological developments worldwide and developing or acquiring new products or new production technology that can be used either to transform existing businesses or to create new ones. Corporate development also seeks to discover new business investment opportunities. The CEO may want to have a corporate development role at Stratum VI to help carry through this long term development work.

There are two different aspects of the work of this role. One is concerned with worldwide networking to keep abreast of developments and of businesses that might potentially be of commercial significance for the organization. The other is directed toward the development of new technological knowledge within the corporation.

If laboratories, for example, are needed for research and development work, they would be subordinate to a Stratum VI corporate development officer. These corporate laboratories would not be concerned with the products that the organization is currently providing (that work belongs to the individual business units), but with the development of those products that the CEO judges are going to be necessary strategically in ten to fifteen years.

Commercial analysis and negotiating staff are needed by the corporate development officer to analyze potential opportunities and secure them for the corporation. The decision to go ahead with any given proposal is determined by the CEO and the corporate executives with sanction by the corporate board.

New Ventures

It is the work of the new ventures function to make the new business opportunities operational within the corporation. The new ventures executive vice president, with the help of a few Stratum V and IV subordinates, builds the starting teams for new units. The selection of the president for the new business unit would be done jointly with the operational executive vice president who will be the eventual recipient of the new unit. When the new business is established and operational, it is handed over to the new ventures group executive vice president. New ventures development work requires close collaboration between this function and the operational executive vice president with whom the business will be placed. The handover process is a gradual one.

Corporate Services

Experience has shown that the provision of services such as legal, accounting, information technology and similar functions can often be combined effectively at the corporate level, resulting in substantial economies. These service functions are not part of the corporation's strategic thrust work, nor are they part of the business operation or future business development work. The issue of centralization versus decentralization applies to these service functions.

The CEO may decide that it is preferable to outsource some services. This has often been the case with information technology work, for example. Or the CEO may judge that to have an effective service, direct accountability within the corporation is required. The optimum balance of providing the services from a central source, allowing business units to provide for themselves or to buy them from outside will vary with changing circumstances such as cost and availability of external services and of competent staff.

Internally provided services can be grouped and run like a business unit, providing services as needed. An executive vice president role for corporate services is sometimes needed, and such a role may be advisable if necessary services are extensive. The persons engaged in corporate services to business units should not be the same people who help the CEO with strategic work. Trying to do this as well as trying to run services at the same time generally does not work well because the focus of the roles are very different.

Headquarter Strategic Staff Functions

There are five functions that relate to the organization's competitive strategic thrust that usually need to work directly for the CEO to support his/her work. These include economic, human and technology resourcing, public affairs and corporate counsel. These five functions are distributed in up to five roles at the executive vice president level.

These are policy development positions whose work is largely direct output support work for the CEO. The people who fill these specialist roles, providing the CEO with strategic advice, should be individuals who like this kind of intellectual work and who do not especially value having large departments to manage. Individuals who value managing large departments can be given departments in business units or in services instead. These large units do not belong in the strategic thrust area.

Corporate Chief Financial Officer

A Stratum VII CEO generally has a chief financial officer at Stratum VI who may have a small subordinate group of Stratum V's and IV's doing financial analysis and keeping in contact with the financial world. This helps the

CEO's strategy development by translating that strategy into financial terms. This function also includes networking in world financial markets.

The CFO is not accountable for bookkeeping and accounting services but is concerned instead with economic resourcing and keeping track of financial conditions from a worldwide perspective. Accounting work belongs in corporate services.

Human Resources Specialist

A staff officer is needed to help with the organizational development of the corporation, with policies in this area and with the talent pool development in the context of long-term corporate strategic plans and societal changes. Again, this role should consist of an individual with just a few subordinates.

The human resources specialist role is not concerned with personnel services such as recruitment, benefits, and salary administration. These services are requisitely done by corporate services or by Human Resources functions within the business units.

Technology Advisor

The person in this role is concerned with the interplay between the commercial consequences of scientific developments and the general trend of new products and production technologies as well as the strategic shape of the future corporation. S/he must develop policies on the technology development work within the corporation.

This function may seem similar to the new business opportunities development role, but the differences in focus make it inefficient to place the work in one role. The technology advisor provides direct output support to the CEO with regard to technology, in close daily interaction with other headquarter colleagues. This is an individual contributor role that should have, at most, a few direct output support subordinates at Stratum V and IV.

Public Affairs

This function involves dealing with governments, networking with other large-scale institutions with respect to possible common interests around strategic issues, and working with customer/client marketing relationships that must be managed 12 to 15 years into the future.

General Corporate Counsel

This role is concerned with strategic consequences of long-term legislative developments and seeks to ensure representation of corporate requirements in new legislation or other government or legal developments.

STRATUM V BUSINESS UNITS & ROLES

At Stratum V, the level of many business units, there are certain functions that arise whether the business units are freestanding Stratum V companies or Stratum V subsidiary companies in larger corporations. The key function of a business unit president is to integrate the interplay between product development, production and marketing/sales in relation to the marketplace, while giving sufficient priority to resource enhancement.

When the business unit is part of a larger corporation, the Stratum V president role serves as an essential connection between the individual business unit operation and the Stratum VII corporate work. One of the reasons that Stratum V appears to be the highest level at which business work ought to be carried out may have to do with the nature of human capability and the fact that Stratum V is the level where people begin to move into borderline areas of the level of complexity of corporate work.

At Stratum V the person has the capability to understand and deal with corporate strategic concepts but is not very far away from the more concrete concerns of Stratum IV general manager level.

Stratum V Mainstream Business Functions

The six mainstream functions are procurement, production, sales, marketing, delivery and product/service development. (The term product is subsequently used to indicate both products and services.) These are the functions that make up the operational spine of the organization. Too often organizations are not clear about the functions that are central to their business and confuse them with support and service functions.

Profit and loss accounting takes place at the business level and has to do with providing products that the marketplace will want: producing or procuring them, selling them to the marketplace and understanding the market in order to continually improve the product. The primary concern of an individual business is with the expenses for providing products to the marketplace and the total revenues from that provision in order to achieve a profit.

These mainstream functions can be aligned in as many Stratum IV roles as are required for the volume of the work. Each of these functions then extends vertically down through Stratum III, II and I as necessary. In some organizations information technology has replaced some or all of the Stratum I roles.

Production and Procurement

Companies provide products for their customers in several ways. Products can be manufactured by the company or can be secured from another organization. Some companies may manufacture their products and procure the materials to do so, while others may need a procurement function that buys the finished products for resale.

An example of a large Stratum IV unit would be a factory of 2000 people headed by a Stratum IV general manager. This factory might have 10 units, each employing 200 people. There would be staff specialists assisting the general manager in the areas of human resources, technology and programming as well as accounting and property and equipment maintenance functions. There would also be ad hoc teams engaged in special projects to seek improved methods of production, productions-flow control and organization structure and staffing.

The production function is the one very often studied and dealt with in conventional organizational theory. However, the mainstream functions of selling, marketing and product development are equally as important in fully achieving organizational goals.

Marketing and Selling

A business organization must be able to deal with the marketplace and provide everything that goes into selling to individual customers. It is necessary to understand what the customer wants, negotiate sales and provide customers with given products at an agreed price.

Marketing is concerned with customers collectively. Marketing functions include market research to determine market needs/desires and promotional campaigns to influence customers to choose the company's products. Marketing also involves continual analysis of pricing structure, distribution, activities of competitors and providing advice to the business unit president based on these analyses.

Sales is concerned with individual customers. Selling includes working with individual customers, helping them decide which product to choose, getting them to buy, arranging for delivery and payment terms and maintaining regular contact with them.

Many organizations sell directly to customers. These may only need a small, spare selling organization if they are dealing with a few very large customers, or they may need a large sales organization if selling to a large diversified market is required. Some organizations need to have a sales force selling to customers throughout the country or in many countries throughout the world while others may sell through distributors, dealers and wholesalers. In many instances selling takes place through a combination of sales channels.

Marketing functions may be mixed with selling or set up separately, depending on organizational requirements. Neither marketing nor selling is senior to the other although one may be more dominant because of the nature of the business. Sales may be more important, for example, where the production of components is for wholesalers and, therefore, marketing has little relevance. Marketing will likely be dominant in mass retailing where such things as advertising, special promotions, packaging, and store and shelf layout are major buying influences.

Confusion sometimes exists in organizations about who 'decides' or who 'owns' prices, discounts, advertising and promotion, customer mix and the like. The CEO of the organization is the person who makes the policy decisions in these areas and who holds the final authority on pricing policy decisions. No other role 'owns' these decisions. Specific decisions are made within marketing and selling in accord with the policies set by the president.

Product/Service Development

A product improvement and development role is not always necessary. It may be possible to do the improvement and development of the company's products and services as part of the marketing function. If it is services that are being provided to the marketplace, a development organization may not be needed. However, in this instance a marketing general manager will likely be needed at Stratum IV who is capable of carrying out market research, who seeks to understand the changing requirements in the marketplace, and who redefines and redevelops the kinds of services that are being provided.

A business unit president who is operating in five- seven- or nine-year thrusts must have subordinates who are capable of helping him/her understand the ever-changing two-, three-, or four-year market requirements and who are capable of doing the development work to ensure that the company is able to cope with the shifting market.

If the company is producing a technical product, there may need to be a Stratum IV product development role with subordinates to help in doing the work. For example, there may be a physical product needing redesign in order to improve it in relation to the evolving market.

Where there is a separate product development function it is preferable to designate it by that title rather than calling it research and development. Research often implies a focus on 'pure science' rather than the commercial focus required of this function in a business setting. The product development function should be in continuing contact with customers and the marketplace. It should also work closely with production, marketing and sales so that their requirements are all taken into consideration.

Product development work for a Stratum V unit should not be confused with the Stratum VI corporate development work. The Stratum VII CEO is concerned with the ten- to fifteen-year business thrust, anticipating what is likely to happen in that period of time, what big competitors are doing, and what scientific and technical breakthroughs are likely to occur. This corporate role involves an understanding of what new products are necessary to modify the nature of the corporation's business units.

Business unit presidents are accountable for ensuring that their existing products are being improved through redesign, development and modification so that the products the business unit is providing are in line with changing market needs.

Business Unit Services

The operational functions of a business unit are the functions by which the business gets done. In addition to the six mainstream business functions there are also necessary resource sustainment, resource enhancement and service functions in support of the operational functions. There is staff specialist work in support of the work of the business unit president as well.

The business unit president may need to provide services such as accounting, human resources, maintenance, information technology, legal counsel and administration for the operational areas. What services are provided and how they are organized in the service unit are dependent upon the requirements of the organization. It is very important to keep in mind that the business is not set up to provide internal services: it is set up to deal with its customers, providing them with products at a profit to the company.

Resource Sustainment Services

There are three main areas where activities may be necessary for a Stratum V business unit to sustain the existing resources. These are finance, general services and maintenance/repair. These services may be grouped under one Stratum IV general manager or be separate if the services are extensive.

Financial Auditing and Services

The financial services provide auditing activities and maintain purchase and sales records, pay accounts, do billing and carry out other activities associated with financial accounting. The accounting function must carry auditing authority to ensure that expenditures fall within the policy limits. However, cost accounting activities generally are carried out by a programming specialist because it is part of advisory work to the president.

General Services

General services may include administrative services such as purchasing, property administration, information technology services and personnel services such as recruitment, interviewing, procedures, training and personnel records and statistics.

Repair and Maintenance Services

Repair and maintenance services may require site workshops at Stratum IV or at Stratum III. If the need for these services is not extensive they may be included under general services.

Stratum V Staff Specialist Functions

The business unit president may need the following staff specialists to assist him or her in business programming, human resources and technology.

Business Programming Specialist

Business programming involves modeling the interplay between the functions of the organization, or exploring various decisions in order to help compare possible courses of action. The business analysis function is called programming. This staff specialist helps the president analyze business plans and priorities by modeling actual and potential markets and sales, production capacities and costs, sales and labor flows, competitor activities and price structure, transportation facilities and costs, work-in-progress and finished goods stock levels and other inventories, cash flows, capital costs, interest rates, foreign exchange and other resource flows affecting business strategies and business success. This ongoing analysis helps to drive long- and short-term business unit planning and the development of new options and helps to optimize the balance between current profitability and longer term survival, development and change.

This Stratum IV role calls for a combination of knowledge and skills in operation research, cost accounting, and process statistics. It requires a substantial business know-how and an understanding of the interdependencies and interactions of product development, material procurement, production, distribution, marketing and sales.

The programming specialist helps the Stratum IV general managers optimize their own programming priorities in relation to the business unit president's plan. The role carries coordinative authority to attempt to sort out differences in priorities and resource demands that may arise between various functions of the unit.

Human Resource Specialist

At Stratum IV the HR specialist helps the president analyze human resource requirements and plans. This assistance includes providing the human resources needed to achieve the strategic plan, monitoring the talent pool and organization development work. It also involves tracking developments in human resource practices, maintaining contact with the corporate human resource policy changes, and recommending human resource policies to strengthen leadership effectiveness and reinforce a constructive climate. The human resource specialist helps the Stratum IV general managers stay within human resource policy in the management and leadership of their people and can give instruction to the general managers in this respect on behalf of the president.

Human resource work needs a practical understanding of all of the work in the organization and a theoretical and practical understanding of managerial hierarchies and how human nature and capability are expressed in them.

Technology Specialist

Information and production technology is concerned with finding ways of optimizing current methods to reduce cost and improve quality, service and delivery. The Stratum IV technology specialist helps the president to ensure the development of technology to achieve continual cost reduction, quality control, increased output and adaptation to requirements for the production of new products.

This work requires ongoing searching for information about new methods being developed in the technical field in order to keep abreast of competitive opportunities. The technical specialist monitors the methods being used, continually re-evaluating them and coming up with ideas for improvement. The new ideas may be in the form of designs for improvements to existing methods or of proposals for development projects to be carried out by task forces. If a project team is formed, the technology specialist monitors its progress. On behalf of the president this specialist may also contract to get work done with corporate technology areas or with outside suppliers.

Resource Enhancement

The business unit president has the accountability to enhance the value of the human and physical resources at his/her disposal. This function is usually carried out by special project teams established under Stratum IV project managers. Examples would be task forces set up to implement a major reorganization or to introduce new production technology.

STRATUM IV GENERAL MANAGERS

Stratum IV general managers of production, sales and marketing and product development may need Stratum III specialist staff in programming, personnel and technology.

For example, a Stratum IV production general manager will often need a programming specialist to act as factory production controller, to help him/her plan, schedule and follow the progress of the factory work flow. This person coordinates the flow of production between units, between suppliers and production, and between production and services such as maintenance and repair.

The human resources specialist would assist the production manager by analyzing and planning human resource requirements and developments. These activities would include planning for personnel changes needed because of changes in the type of work or in technology, planning for recruitment or retraining, monitoring and coordination of human resource practices of colleagues at Stratum III, maintaining contact with business unit human resources on HR policies and recommending any changes needed for improvement.

A technology specialist may be needed to keep the general manager up-to-date on the latest information technology advances or advances in production technology.

STRATUM III MUTUAL RECOGNITION UNITS (MRUs)

In organizations where there is extensive first line work as in a factory where the direct output is at Stratum I, mutual recognition units (MRUs) generally need to be established. MRUs are units of up to 200-250 people with a maximum of 300.

The reason for the maximum of 300 is the discovery that up to that number it is possible for the Stratum III MRU manager to carry through his or her function (service providing, manufacturing or production) in a unit in which everybody can recognize everyone else. That mutual recognition is lost when numbers get above the 250-300 level.

For many years it was thought necessary to have so-called small factories because they seemed to work better than large ones. That does not appear to be necessary. What seems to be important is that factories or large-scale service organizations be organized at Stratum III in mutual recognition units. The Stratum III MRU breaks the Stratum IV general managerial organization, where there are large numbers of employees, into units that are small enough for people to recognize each other and there is a feeling that everyone is working in the same place. This provides a sense of cohesiveness in the shop and office services floor areas that gives a sound basis for effective managerial leadership at the first line managerial level in relation to operating, clerical and service-providing personnel. These MRUs have a Stratum III MRU manager with first line managers at Stratum II and then Stratum I operators and clerks.

MRU Specialist Staff

The MRU manager may need programming and service specialists, especially if it is, for example, a production department. The MRU will not need an HR specialist because the maximum number of subordinates does not provide enough work for such a full time role.

With regard to programming it may be useful for the MRU manager to have specialist staff such as technicians at Stratum II who can help with scheduling, technical, or manufacturing process problems as they come up. It must be absolutely clear, however, that production accountability is in the operational managerial line.

A Stratum II technology staff specialist may be needed to assist the Stratum III unit manager to sustain unbroken production flows by providing on-site methods for overcoming unforeseen obstacles and by preventing such obstacles by anticipating them.

FIRST LINE UNITS

In many organizations, or in specific units of an organization, first line employees produce much of the output. In organizations that have first line units, a large percentage of the employees are found in Stratum I roles. Because these units have a large impact on the organization, its human resources, its output and its bottom line, the factors involved in managing first line units are dealt with extensively in this chapter.

Managing these units effectively can substantially:

- improve the work environment
- enhance employee satisfaction
- increase productivity and profits

A first line unit is composed of a first line manager (FLM) and all of his/her subordinates. In the following sections the role of the first line manager is described along with the accountability and authority of this role. Issues in managing first line units when shifts are necessary are also discussed. The material will focus on Stratum I first line work with the First Line Manager at Stratum II, since this is where most first line work is found.

Three Common Problems Found in First Line Units

Three common problems are frequently found in organizations that have first line units:

1. First line employees do not have *one* clearly designated manager.

They may have a 'supervisor' who has only partial managerial accountability and authority. This person is usually not Stratum II capable, but rather is a more experienced or higher level Stratum I. Sometimes there is no Stratum II manager at all, with the first full managerial role found at Stratum III. In situations where shifts are required, a Stratum II manager is sometimes assigned to the day shift with 'supervisors' handling the 2nd and 3rd shifts. Often there are 'supervisors' on each shift with 'their people'. However, no one is accountable for the area or activity as a whole.

The result is that in many organizations first line employees are given assignments by several different persons who are in quasi-managerial positions above them. Employees are then unclear about their work priorities, about who is accountable for their work and what person to go to when they need help.

2. There is a lack of clear accountability for the results of the work and the working behavior of first line employees.

When a number of different roles are given partial accountability for the oversight of first line workers, it becomes difficult to hold any given individual accountable for results of their work other than the employees themselves. In this situation first line employees are held accountable for results that are outside their control and get unfairly blamed for things that go wrong.

3. There are no clearly specified managerial practices for first line managers to carry out in working with their subordinates.

When there is not a clearly specified Stratum II first line manager, or where there are a variety of people supervising the first line, some managerial practices such as planning, task assignment, coaching and appraisal are done by different individuals, if indeed they are done at all. The result is a lack of clarity. No single immediate manager is accountable for equipment, maintenance and improvements. There is no manager who can be held accountable for the results.

Addressing These Problems Requisitely

With the use of requisite organization principles and practices, organizations can significantly improve the operation of their first line units. The first steps to address the problems described above are to:

- establish Stratum II first line manager roles
- institute requisite management practices to be carried out by this manager

Establish Stratum II First Line Manager Roles

First line manager (FLM) roles need to be established at Stratum II. These roles should carry accountability and authority for the results of the work and working behavior of their Stratum I first line subordinates, for all the financial and physical resources and for process improvements. The FLM may have one or more assistants in Stratum I roles if required by the work, but these are not managerial roles.

Institute Requisite Management Practices

Managers at all levels throughout the organization, including first line managers, should carry out management practices.

The First Line Manager Role

Some of the reasons given by organizations as to why supervisors or assistant managers are needed rather than a full scale, fully accountable manager are:

- there are a large number of people to be 'supervised'
- some of the work may need to be done outside normal working hours
- continuing training is required
- the work has to be done in geographically dispersed areas
- facilities, machines and equipment have to be continuously maintained

In many organizations the response to these issues is to provide assistance to first line manager roles by a more experienced worker of Stratum I capability. Sometimes one or even two quasi-managerial roles are established above the first line employee. In such instances employees do not know whose directions they should follow when they get conflicting instructions.

For example, in one organization there were 105 first line workers below a first line manager. This unit was divided into five smaller groups, each headed by an 'associate' manager. Below each 'associate' manager were work coordinators, each handling five to eight first line workers. Situations such as this often exist because the response to the growth of a first line unit is to add layers below the first line manager rather than splitting the unit and adding one or more additional first line managers in order to deal with span of control issues.

Stratum I first line employees usually have a good sense of who their real manager is even when there are intervening roles such as supervisor, assistant manager and work coordinator. They know to whom they should go to get their problems resolved.

If, as is sometimes the case, the first full managerial role is not found until a role at Stratum III, this person is not readily accessible to the first line worker. In these instances there is also too large a gap in capability between that of the first line worker and this manager. To be fully effective in their work, first line workers need a Stratum II first line manager.

Examine the Current Situation

It can be helpful to get a picture of the situation as it currently exists in an organization. There are a number of ways to do this.

One way to determine whether or not there is a Stratum II first line manager is to ask first line workers who their manager is. Often there will be two or three different answers within one work group. One organization was surprised when several employees said that they *did not know* who their manager was.

If there appear to be several roles managing first line employees, find out which role carries out appraisals and which decides merit increases. Sometimes employees are told, apologetically, that the work coordinator does the appraisals because it would be too onerous for the manager to do so since there are so many first line workers, but that the merit increase is determined by the first line manager.

Consider the titles. Myriad titles such as supervisor, assistant manager, associate manager, lead and work coordinator are often found. When these titles are used, it usually indicates that the role is not one that carries full managerial accountability and authority. This is even more evident if more than one role with these titles exists.

Multiple Layers between the Manager and the First Line Worker

When questioned as to why extra layers exist between the manager and the first line, a number of answers are often provided. One reason given is that career paths are needed to motivate first line workers. Another reason is that in order to move an individual up a grade to increase their compensation another role needed to be created, such as assistant or associate manager. Another reason is to aid in retention—that it seemed necessary to provide a role for someone who had grown in capability or who had been in a role for a long time in order to retain them for the organization. Or the first line unit has grown too large to be handled by the manager alone.

Another reason, frequently found but rarely discussed, is that the manager shown on the organization chart is not capable of managing the unit and needs one or more 'assistant' managers to shore him or her up in an attempt to get the work done.

In an organization that is requisitely structured there will not be managerial and subordinate roles within the same stratum. Where there is such a 'jam-up' of roles within a stratum, called role compression, resentment and frustration build up and resources are ineffectively used.

Clarifying the First Line Manager Role

The starting place for clarifying a first line unit is to establish an FLM section and role. This role carries the same accountability and authority as any other managerial role in the organization. It is a full managerial role, not that of a 'supervisor'.

The level of work of the first line manager role is in Stratum II, with the longest task(s) assigned to the role needing to be completed at somewhere from three months to one year. The type of complexity of information processing required by the individual in the role will be cumulative, that is the individual will be able to diagnose problems and in this way add value to his/her subordinates by helping solve their problems and by providing context for their work.

By contrast, the longest tasks or task sequences assigned to Stratum I roles need to be completed somewhere between one day and three months. The type of complexity required by individuals in these roles is the ability to follow a clearly prescribed pathway to the end goal. There is usually a hands-on component to the work.

Span of Control

How many first line employees an FLM can manage is a function of the work that needs to get done. An FLM may be able to manage from as few as five or so to perhaps as many as 60 or 70 subordinates, depending on the circumstances.

Variables that need to be considered in determining how many subordinates an FLM can reasonably manage include:

- whether or not shifts are involved
- physical location of subordinates
- diversity and complexity of the work
- how much direct output work the manager personally has to do
- how many meetings are required
- whether or not assistant roles can be assigned

A major consideration here is the number of subordinates for whom the FLM can fully carry out the requisite managerial practices described above. In particular this means that FLMs must know all of their subordinates well enough to be able to judge their individual personal effectiveness and coach and develop them as required.

For example, the FLM might be able to handle a group of first line subordinates toward the larger end of the range when all work takes place during normal working hours in one area, few meetings are needed, all workers do similar work in relatively unvarying conditions and the manager has an assistant to handle the administrative work.

Providing Assistance to the First Line Manager

The first line manager may need one or more assistants in order to get the work done. These may be full time assistants called First Line Manager Assistants (FLMA) or they may be part-time specialist subordinates who have specific support roles. How many of these roles are required and what these roles are assigned to do is a function of the work that needs to get done.

First Line Manager Assistants

The FLM may need one or more first line manager assistants (FLMAs) to help him or her to carry out the work of the unit. These are Stratum I employees who are assigned administrative, technical, scheduling or training work depending upon what is required. These are generally full time roles filled by individuals who have experience working in the unit.

The FLMA role is established to assist the FLM meet his/her accountabilities in some of the following ways:

- Assigning tasks within guidelines provided by the FLM
- Doing special training of colleague-subordinates as assigned by the FLM
- Maintaining an environment of cooperative working to accomplish all of the assigned work of the team
- Carrying out specifically assigned tasks with regard to administrative, maintenance, scheduling and technical outputs as direct output support to the FLM
- Monitoring working behavior and adherence to safety procedures
- Taking immediate action to deal with serious infractions of policies or regulations

FLMAs are not managers, and the role carries no accountability for carrying out management practices. FLMAs may or may not make recommendations to the FLM on the effectiveness of their colleagues depending on the situation and how the role needs to be established.

Specialist Operators in Part-time Support Roles

The first line manager may need only part-time specialist support from designated operators to help with administrative, technical, scheduling and training issues. When employees have a problem they can seek help from the relevant specialist whose role is given this accountability and authority. This person would stop what he or she is doing to deal with the issue. (These specialist roles can only be created when the work of the role can be interrupted to provide the needed assistance.) When not engaged in their specialist work, individuals in these roles carry out their regularly assigned first line work.

Problems requiring assistance might include equipment that is not working correctly, resources that are missing, not understanding the process, confusion as to priorities and so on. For example, one production facility has regular turnover because of its undesirable location and difficult physical working conditions. A skilled operative who enjoys training others has been appointed training specialist. There are new employees almost every week. Whenever a newly hired person needs reinforcement or clarification of the basic training they received before starting their job, the training specialist is right there on the floor to help them.

Involvement of Stratum III Managers

The Stratum III manager has the accountability and authority to provide the first line units for whose output s/he is accountable with a satisfactory working environment, including the physical and technological resources needed to achieve the assigned tasks. S/he also provides the human resources required, authorizing the necessary roles and determining where those roles are placed in Stratum I. This may be at high, mid or low within the stratum depending on the level of work required. This manager analyzes what support is needed by the FLM in training, scheduling and technical areas and establishes any Stratum I first line manager assistant or specialist roles that may be required.

The Stratum III manager also determines if Stratum II specialist roles are needed for the entire Stratum III unit. For example a Stratum II administrator or a deputy for Stratum III manager may be needed to handle emergency situations on shifts where the first line manager is not present.

Stratum III managers review their FLMs' managerial leadership work carrying out the practices described above, ensuring evenness and fairness of treatment of the FLMs' subordinates. The Stratum III manager also provides mentoring and individual development discussions to first line employees outside their present role. The Stratum III manager is accountable for ensuring that the FLMs work together in a manner that contributes to the successful achievement of the assigned output of the Stratum III unit.

The Stratum III Mutual Recognition Unit

This Stratum III manager is in charge of a Mutual Recognition Unit (MRU) in which s/he can recognize all the Stratum I and Stratum II employees. As mentioned earlier, MRUs are most effective if they are not larger than 250 to 300 people, a number that appears to be the outside limit where it is possible for everyone in the group to recognize each other. This number provides an outside limit that a Stratum III manager can handle.

Stratum IV General or Functional Manager

The Stratum IV general or functional manager (GM) is held accountable by the Stratum V business unit CEO for ensuring that the site or department has effective, well-led MRUs that can produce the required output and continuously improve the way that output is achieved. S/he is accountable for translating the business unit goals into a direction that guides the operation in the site or department and for communicating that direction to everyone within it. From time to time the GM will hold three-level meetings to communicate directly with an entire group as needed.

GMs will not know first line employees personally but will shape the culture in which they work by the systems and practices they put in place and by their own actions and example. The GM is accountable for the processes used and for integrating the output of his/her mutual recognition units.

GMs provide leadership in significant site-wide or department-wide changes that influence the working environment at the FLM level. They lead the annual or semi-annual review of the human resources in the division to ensure the timeliness of judgments and the adequacy of talent pool development and succession management activities. As their Managers-once-Removed, GMs have specific accountability for mentoring and the individual development of the FLMs and other employees in Stratum II roles.

The number of first line units that are needed and can be resourced in an MRU is the decision of the GM. The GM will also be involved in preparing any slate of candidates provided to the MRU manager from which to select FLMs. The MRU manager will make the actual selection and is not to be required to take anyone whom s/he does not believe capable of doing the work in the role.

In one organization, the first line work that needed to be done at Stratum I was reviewed. The two layers between the FLM and his/her subordinates were removed and their roles were replaced by FLMAs and support specialists. When the number of people involved was reviewed by the GM, it became evident that an additional Stratum III MRU was needed.

Selecting First Line Managers

In selecting individuals for the first line manager role there are three major considerations:

- Do they have the necessary complexity of information processing at Stratum II to do the work of the role?
- Do they value the role? Do they want to manage other people?
- Do they have or can they acquire the necessary skilled knowledge to successfully carry out the role? (New FLMs should be trained for the role before they undertake it.)

All too often someone who has superior technical knowledge and skills is put in an FLM role without considering their complexity of information processing and/or their commitment to being a manager.

Special Circumstances in First Line Units

Managing first line work may involve the special situations of trade unions and the need for shifts.

Trade Unions

There is a tendency to regard subordinates at Stratum I who are trade union members as different, to feel that they can't become members of the company, that they have to be treated with kid gloves, and that there cannot be effective managerial leadership of people who are trade union members. This is an important misconception.

It is extremely important that the unit manager make clear to first line managers that the trade union agreements and arrangements are matters between the union and higher management and that subordinates are subordinates. They are operators for whose work and working behavior their managers are accountable. Their managers have to meet with them, have to pull them together into an effective working team, and have to ensure that they are getting effective collaborative working relationships between them.

Where a site or a department is union organized, the FLM must understand and work within negotiated agreements. What can and often happens is that the union members develop local customs and practices that they treat as though they were union agreements. They may implement practices that their union would like to negotiate, or embrace ideologies, political programs or values associated with their union membership, producing inflexible or restrictive practices that, once established, are difficult to eradicate. The FLM must work to prevent such practices or to eliminate them if they occur.

Multiple Shifts

Shifts may be necessary to handle the work flow. Issues involved when shifts are needed are addressed in the sections that follow.

First Line Shifts

There are two important findings from requisite consultative research that improve work on shifts, in addition to having a clearly accountable Stratum II manager for each employee on each shift. These are:

- One first line manager should be accountable for all shifts in a geographical area or a specific function
- First line employees are often able to organize their own work and can be relied on to carry it forward without the need for direct supervision throughout every shift

These two findings apply whether there are three shifts covering 24/7 or just extended working hours with one and a half or two shifts in a 24-hour period.

One First Line Manager Accountable for all Shifts in an Area

First line units should be established with one Stratum II first line manager in charge of one clearly defined geographical/physical area or a specific function for all shifts in a 24-hour period. The FLM is accountable for using the physical and human resources to obtain optimum results from his/her area 24 hours a day or for however long the shifts last. In this way the best possible results are obtained.

With one person accountable for a specified area, for example, the usual maintenance and equipment difficulties are no longer a problem. A malfunctioning machine will be attended to and not left for the next shift. The first line manager in charge of that area sees to it that things are taken care of since accountability is clear.

One company that has 250 people per shift decided to establish eight first line manager roles, replacing 25 team leaders. They divided the geographical territory for the full 24 hours of three shifts among the eight first line managers. Once they determined what would be most workable, territories were established by making demarcations on the floor. By doing this they achieved clarity of managerial accountability and cut manpower costs substantially. A significant increase in productivity resulted within a few weeks along with a large reduction in turnover.

Managing Multiple Shifts

In order to manage multiple shifts, FLMs need to arrange their schedules so that they come in half an hour early to be present for the end of the night shift and then work briefly into the second shift. In this way they are there for the work hand-over and are in touch on a daily basis with all three shifts. Where only two shifts are necessary the manager stays briefly for the hand-over. When the manager cannot be on hand for the shift hand-over someone acting on his or her behalf, such as a scheduling specialist operator, arranges the hand-over and schedules new tasks.

FLMs also need to arrange to work several hours into the evening and come in a few hours early for the night shift several times a month. From time to time FLMs also need to work part or all of the weekend shifts, particularly if there are individuals who only work on weekends. This gives employees who work those shifts the opportunity to have sufficient access to their manager and gives the manager the opportunity to keep in contact with all his/her subordinates.

This varied scheduling is also necessary so that FLMs can stay in close touch with all of their subordinates in order to judge their effectiveness from continuing first hand knowledge and to coach them as appropriate. The FLM evaluates employees' effectiveness individually by accumulating information over periods of days and weeks without having to watch them continuously as they work during each shift

FLMs will want to arrange to get all of their subordinates together for meetings on a regular basis, possibly for an hour every two or three weeks. In many cases this will require paying overtime. These full group meetings are a necessary part of providing context to the group as a whole about goals and results and are the way the manager binds the group together as a cohesive unit.

Subordinates Can Often Direct Their Own Work on Shifts

One of the reasons that additional layers of management have been added between the real manager and first line employees is the mistaken belief that there needs to be a full scale manager on hand for each shift if the operators are to do any work. In fact, employees on shift can be expected to work together under the ordinary conditions of collateral (cooperative) relationships between work colleagues. Such an arrangement does, however, require that clearly organized tasks can be assigned and that operating conditions are likely to be reliable for the whole shift.

Shifts other than the day shift often do not have many of the technical, scheduling and training support activities and services ordinarily available during the day. Individuals in specialist roles who have the knowledge and authority and experience to know what to do, may have to be available to provide the required assistance in these areas. Having such individuals on hand often allows evening, night and weekend shifts to operate effectively without their FLM on site.

Directing their own work when the circumstances are suitable allows employees the opportunity to use their full capability.

Handling Serious Problems on Shifts

In circumstances where Stratum I employees on shifts can do their own work without a FLM on hand throughout the whole shift, provision needs to be made, and all employees need to know what to do, in case of emergency. Emergencies can include such things as serious illness or accidents, fighting, drunkenness or drug use, serious mechanical breakdowns and so on.

There are many possible ways to plan ahead for handling such situations. One of the easiest solutions is for the FLM to be available by phone or for a number of FLMs whose work is related to take turns being on call. In instances where there are a number of first line managers in a related area, one FLM can be scheduled to be on hand on each shift.

Another way of handling the problem is for the Stratum III or Stratum IV manager to have a full time deputy on each shift to cover that manager's whole area. A deputy role is of great importance when there are serious risks of danger, as, for example, in mining operations or chemical plants. The deputy role is usually a role one stratum below that of the manager. The role does not carry managerial accountability and authority and does not provide input into personal effectiveness appraisals.

The deputy is authorized to act for his/her manager, with the manager's authority. In the manager's absence, the deputy can issue instructions to deal with the types of situations described above.

For example, in organizations with a number of small night shifts located in widely separated locations, the MoR may determine that the shifts could manage their own work if two conditions were met: their FLMs had to be there for the hand-over, and a deputy to the MoR had to be available to respond to and, if necessary, travel to any area that was having a problem.

Self-Managed Teams are not Appropriate

There is an important difference between a shift where employees direct their own work and self-managed teams. In the former case there is a first line manager accountable for the output of each first line worker. In self-managed teams the idea is that the group of employees is supposed to be accountable as a team.

Setting up self-managed teams undercuts the authority of the manager. Can the first line manager hold the team accountable for its work? How do you hold a group accountable? Do they get evaluated as a group or deselected as a group? What happens if the manager involved does not believe the work is going on satisfactorily? What happens if there is a disagreement between manager and the team or a team's spokesperson? Where does the authority lie?

Establishing self-managed teams is often a response to a situation where there is lack of effective managerial leadership or where there is no belief in the possibility of effective management. While there is sometimes a short term 'honeymoon' effect after setting up self-directing teams on the shop floor, such teams are not a medium-term or a long-term answer to the need for clear accountability and managerial leadership. Self-managing teams run into real trouble because it is impossible to determine who has accountability for what. They are usually eliminated after a relatively short period of time.

The correct approach is to set up the conditions for effective managerial leadership throughout the whole system, from top to bottom, and to hold managers accountable for getting the required work done. In a requisite organization fully authorized and accountable first line managerial roles are established at Stratum II, where the unit managers hold the first line managers accountable for effective leadership of their first line personnel. There are no self-managed teams.

Determining the Requisite Structure for Shifts

Reorganizing first line units generally requires analysis of the work that is to be done. The units need to be designed so that the FLM can develop effective face-to-face relationships with individual subordinates. Where there are shifts, how geographical territories might best be structured needs to be thought through.

When a full Stratum II FLM role is established, it does not necessarily mean that the work being done by the quasi-managerial roles goes away, although often a substantial amount of duplication can be eliminated.

The work required needs to be carefully considered and sufficient roles need to be in place to get it done.

The basic question is always "what is the work we need to get done and how can that best happen?" In some cases the answer to this may involve establishing one or more additional first line units, while in other instances there may need to be a first line manager assistant or specialist roles or both.

Some of the questions that FLM managers working with their Stratum III MRU manager will want to consider include:

- How can the work best be divided up geographically so that a discrete area is under one FLM for a 24-hour shift?
- Does the structure of related units need to be reorganized?
- What is the amount of work on the different shifts? For example, the night shift may be relatively quiet, the weekend shift may also be quite slow or it may be the busiest shift of all. Does the structure of related units need to be reorganized?
- If the employees on shift are in separate locations, how can this best be handled?
- How many employees are needed on each shift? This number may vary widely based on the workflow.
- What kind of assistance is needed on shifts when the FLM is not on site? When the FLM is on site? Administration? Training? Technical? Work Coordination? Does this work have to be full time or can the person filling the role do first line work and provide specialist advice on a part-time, as-needed basis? Can the role combine administrative and training work? Technical expertise and training? How do these needs differ on different shifts?
- What kind of safety and/or maintenance expertise is needed?
- Can the administrative work be done largely on the day shift or is it necessary to some extent on all shifts?
- What types of problems that need attention typically arise on shifts? Can one FLM be deputized to handle several first line units on the 2nd or 3rd shifts? Should a deputy for the Stratum

III or Stratum IV manager be on hand because of the potential severity of the problems?

Benefits of Establishing Requisite First line Units

Establishing requisite first line managers at Stratum II and organizing shifts requisitely require substantial analysis of the work and the situation. The implementation of requisite conditions of accountability, authority, management practices and organization design are the best guarantee that first line employees can and will take their place as reliable, involved employees with high morale. They will not be alienated, disappointed people punished for results they cannot control, but will feel part of an organization that manages them appropriately and where they get satisfaction from using their full capability.

Chapter 5

MANAGEMENT PRACTICES

The requisite principles presented in this book underlie the managerial practices described in this chapter. These practices include both senior management practices with regard to creating the organization's vision, values and culture and the practices of all managers in relation to their immediate subordinates. Requisite leadership practices can be clearly described and can be taught, which enable these practices to be established and managers to be held accountable for carrying them out.

ORGANIZATIONAL LEADERSHIP PRACTICES

The head of an organization is accountable to provide and communicate the vision for the organization as a whole and to oversee the organization's values and culture. The leader establishes a sense of common purpose throughout the organization and sets the overarching conditions within which the employees can understand how to move together in the same direction.

Communicating the Vision

Communicating the vision of what is to be accomplished is an essential task of the leader of any organization whether it is a corporation consisting of multiple business units, an individual business unit, a factory or a department. Anyone who heads a unit must have in mind and must communicate the vision for that unit on a continuing basis. This vision must be communicated to all members of the unit at one time, whether 80, 8,000 or 80,000 people are involved. This is now possible through the use of technology such as video conferencing. The vision is not communicated to immediate subordinates who then communicate it further down to their subordinates: this practice leads to inaccuracy and distortion of the message.

In a Stratum VII corporation the CEO will provide a vision for the corporation in a 20- to 30-year time frame, outlining where s/he, in conjunction with the board, sees the organization heading. In a Stratum V company or business unit the vision will be developed and presented in a five- to seven-year outlook and in a smaller Stratum IV company the outreach of the vision will be somewhere between two to five years.

Corporate Culture

In his early work with organizations, Elliott Jaques identified and named the concept of 'corporate culture'. Corporate culture consists of a company's values, its rules and regulations, policies and procedures, customs and practices, its traditions, beliefs and assumptions and its common language. Corporate culture can be thought of as 'the way we do things around here'.

Corporate culture can be described, can be dealt with and can be changed. Organizational leaders can and must have the ability to modify aspects of corporate culture as part of the process of achieving the organization's goals.

For example, corporate cultures change when new technology is introduced. A new technology usually involves changing procedures and establishing new policies. The process often adds to the common corporate language. Just how the introduction of a given technology will change the culture can and should be considered and managed by the organization's leaders.

Corporate Values

The principles of Requisite Organization deal with such corporate values as justice and equity, the opportunity for appeal, fair pay, and equal opportunity to use one's full capability. Corporate values exist whether they are articulated or not. They are expressed in the organization's policies and demonstrated in its practices. The values a corporation espouses and demonstrates require the attention of the organization's leader. S/he must continually review how the organization is doing things to ensure that it is in line with the overall values of the company.

The behavior of the organization's leader also has to be consistent with the corporate values. Trust and confidence are built when corporate systems are congruent with the stated values of the company and the leader's behavior and practices are consistently in line with these systems.

Contradiction is sensed by everyone and is a very substantial source of mistrust. For example, a leader may say that he wants all employees to have a balanced life with adequate time for family, friends and outside activities, but in reality people know that they will need to put in 10- to 12-hour days on a regular basis if they wish to be successful.

Society's Values

The organization's leader has to understand the values of the society or societies in which the company is operating and, within reason, the company has to work within those values. Values in Japan and Saudi Arabia are quite different from those in the United States, for example. The challenge is to understand the differences and, insofar as possible, to operate effectively in different societies while keeping values consistent with the overall company values and philosophy—no small challenge for the leaders of global corporations.

Private Values

An individual's private values are his or her own business. However, as part of the employment contract, employees must behave in line with the corporate values by adhering to the requirements of corporate policies and procedures.

MANAGEMENT LEADERSHIP PRACTICES FOR ALL MANAGERS

All managerial roles in all functions at all levels in a requisite organization carry direct leadership accountability and authority with regard to subordinates. For this reason the term managerial leadership is used throughout in requisite work.

Requisite structure provides the basis for managerial leadership by selecting managers who are one level of capability higher than their subordinates. This gives the organization managers who are capable of working with a wider view of situations than their subordinates and who can set necessary and sufficient context for them, delegate tasks appropriately and make good judgments of personal effectiveness.

The essence of managerial leadership accountability is to enable subordinates to work together in such a way that each person can get on with his or her own work, knowing where the whole group is heading. In this way everyone moves along together and the desired outcomes are achieved.

Managerial Accountability

Managerial accountability and authority were described in Chapter One. These concepts are reviewed here because they form the basis for requisite Management Practices.

Managers are held accountable, by their managers, for:

- the work and working behavior of their subordinates and for the overall unit/department results
- exercising managerial leadership by carrying out the required Management Practices
- building and sustaining their group of subordinates as an effective team
- their own personal effectiveness

Minimum Managerial Authority

In order to be held accountable for the work of their subordinates, managers need certain minimum authority with regard to immediate subordinates. This includes the authority to:

- veto the selection of a candidate they deem unsuitable for a subordinate role
- decide the assignment of tasks to their subordinates
- conduct personal effectiveness appraisals and decide pay within policy parameters
- initiate removal from role of a subordinate whom they deem unable to do the work of a role

Essential Management Practices

There are a number of simple, straightforward Management Practices for which all managers are accountable. Experienced managers for the most part are familiar with these practices and know that they are necessary. For a variety of reasons many organizations do not hold managers accountable for carrying out all of these practices. One of the major reasons is that they do not have the requisite processes to enable and require them to be practiced.

In a requisite organization they must all be carried out. They are foundational to establishing clarity and trust and achieving increased effectiveness and productivity. These managerial practices include:

1. **Managerial Planning**—Determining how to achieve the goals of the unit

2. **Context Setting**—Regular updating of the background within which the work must be carried out

3. **Task Assignment**—Assigning tasks specifying quality, quantity, target completion time and resources available

4. **Managerial Coaching**—Helping individual subordinates to be able to carry out the full range of work in their role

5. **Personal Effectiveness Appraisal**—Judging how well each subordinate is working and discussing it with him/her on a regular basis

6. **Merit Review**—Annual evaluation of applied capability with a decision on compensation adjustment within policy

7. **Selection**—Practices for filling roles and choosing new subordinates

8. **Induction**—Introducing an employee to a new role and to the unit

9. **Deselection and Dismissal**—Processes for removing an employee from role

10. **Managerial Meetings**—Regular meetings with all immediate subordinates

11. **Continual Improvement**—Seeking to improve processes that the manager controls

The first three Management Practices, planning, setting context and assigning tasks, were covered in depth in Chapter Three. In this chapter the remaining eight practices are described.

COACHING

Coaching is the process by which a manager helps subordinates to understand the full range of their individual roles, what they need to do to perform the work of that role effectively, and what they need to do in order to develop in that role. The coaching of subordinates is an ordinary part of every manager's regular activities and an essential part of a manager's continuing review of each subordinate's personal effectiveness.

In order to guide the development of a subordinate in his/her current role, the manager must have a sense of the rate of growth of that person's future potential. With this in mind, the manager seeks to provide work experiences that are consistent with that growth, providing any coaching, teaching and training necessary. The outcome from regular and appropriate coaching is continual improvement in the effectiveness of employees in their roles and the release of each employee's full capability. Managers are accountable to be proactive coaches.

Teaching and training are part of the coaching process. In order to clarify terminology that has multiple meanings, the term **teaching is** used in Requisite Organization work to describe **the imparting of knowledge to individuals by lectures and discussions.** The term **training is** used to describe **the process of helping individuals to develop or enhance their skills through practice, either on the job or through learning simulations.** Skill that has been developed through training enables individuals to use their knowledge in problem-solving activities without having to reconstruct many of the routine decisions involved, thus freeing up the use of their judgment for other problem-solving activities.

Purposes of Coaching

The purposes of coaching are to help subordinates to:

- understand the full range of opportunities in their individual roles and what they need to do to take advantage of those opportunities
- add to their knowledge and skills
- share the manager's knowledge, skills and experience
- more fully understand, and hence be able to bring their behavior more in line with, corporate values and corporate philosophy
- be aware of any behavior that may become dysfunctional at work if it continues

Coaching does not involve trying to change a subordinate's values or personality, since that is neither a concern of the manager nor of the organization. If there are major personality problems, the manager must make it clear to the subordinate that continuation of the problem behavior is unacceptable. If the situation warrants it, the manager should make time available for a subordinate to seek off-site, professional counseling, if s/he wishes to do so.

In coaching subordinates, a manager is concerned with their capability to perform the full range of work within their current roles. The manager is seeking to get work done by his/her subordinates in an effective and productive way and to enable subordinates to use their abilities fully in doing their work.

Counseling

Counseling by the manager is done when someone asks for advice with a personal problem. Managers can give counsel in general terms. For example, "What someone else I know did with such a problem was this . . ." or, "You might think about the possibility of . . .". If this type of assistance is not adequate, subordinates should be referred for professional help if the situation is sufficiently serious.

Coaching Triggers

Managers will find that the need for coaching occurs as a normal by-product of work assignments, periodic reviews of progress and the ongoing personal effectiveness appraisal process.

There are five major reasons for coaching:

- person new to the role
- progress toward achieving assigned tasks
- the need to strengthen existing skills and knowledge
- readiness for development within the current role
- specific difficulties identified by the manager or subordinate

Person New to the Role

In addition to induction activities and orientation to their new role, new employees or employees in a new role usually need coaching, in order to understand what is expected.

Progress Toward Achieving Assigned Tasks

A subordinate's work toward achieving his or her assigned tasks may be slower or faster than required by the manager. In either event, this situation needs to be reviewed, adjustments made to work plans, and help given to the subordinate as needed.

The Need to Strengthen Existing Skills and Knowledge

Managers, both in the appraisal process and normal activities such as work assignments and meetings, will often identify areas of subordinates' skills and knowledge that need strengthening or improving.

Readiness for Development within Current Role

When a manager observes that a subordinate is ready for development within his or her current role, the manager discusses this with the individual and arranges the necessary activities to enable that development. Subordinates may also request developmental opportunities. In this event the manager determines, in discussion with the employee, whether or not the person is ready for that step and whether or not it is appropriate for the organization.

Specific Difficulties

Managerial coaching should take place whenever a subordinate is experiencing difficulties. This type of coaching must not be delayed until a performance review. Managers should also ask subordinates to identify areas where they may be having problems.

Problems may be related to the manager's task formulation and assignment process. For example, the goals may be too complex for the level of the subordinate's capability. There may also be difficulties regarding methods, resources, procedures or limits. These are matters to be sorted out in discussions between the manager and the subordinate. Problems may be associated with the nature of ongoing working relationships. Often these types of problems stem from the need to adjust the cross-functional accountabilities and authorities of the subordinate's role in relation to other roles.

A subordinate's temperament may cause problems. Managers need to handle such situations judiciously. As mentioned earlier, it is not the business of the manager to try to change the personality of any subordinate. It is appropriate, however, for the manager to point out the need for behavioral changes in areas where the person's temperament interferes with his/her ability to get work done. Employees should be referred for counseling if necessary.

Effective Managerial Coaching

Coaching consists of discussing with subordinates where the manager believes them to be working at the present time in terms of capability, their potential in their current role, and the things they are not able to achieve at the moment. This clarity enables the manager to provide training to ensure that subordinates increase their skilled knowledge so that they can increase their applied capability and work more effectively.

As the manager identifies opportunities for growth in a subordinate's current role or deficiencies in the subordinate's performance, s/he should set aside sufficient time to discuss these issues with the subordinate as part of the ongoing coaching process. The manager indicates what the subordinate needs to learn in terms of knowledge or greater skill to improve his/her work performance, to overcome weaknesses or to solve problems.

Arising out of such a discussion, or as part of it, the manager might teach or train the individual, or arrange for teaching or training by others. As part of coaching, managers share with subordinates knowledge and skills gained from their own work experiences.

The subordinate must value this teaching, training and/or experience sharing if it is to be effective. If the subordinate does not value certain kinds of new knowledge and skills and does not benefit from the coaching, this must be taken into account when discussing his/her progress in the current role.

Coaching is one of the ways in which managers add value to their subordinates' work. It can be a time consuming process, but it is central to building subordinate confidence, loyalty and sense of teamwork and getting the work of the group done. If a subordinate is not performing satisfactorily, it is not only a problem of the person involved but of the manager as well, since it is part of the manager's accountability to provide sufficient coaching to enable subordinates to be successful in their roles.

MoR's Role in the Coaching Process

The full performance of the coaching process cannot be left to managerial choice and goodwill. MoRs must see to it that their subordinates who are managers actually do coach on a continuing basis. To that end, MoRs must themselves act as appropriate role models by fully and effectively discharging their coaching accountabilities with their own subordinates. MoRs must also judge their immediate subordinates' effectiveness in coaching their own subordinates.

PERSONAL EFFECTIVENESS APPRAISAL

Managers are accountable for judging the effectiveness of their subordinates in doing their work. No performance can be quantified: all of the appraisal of performance is based on the manager's judgment of how well subordinates handle the available resources and the impact of unexpected events. These judgments are some of the most important decisions managers make in terms of managerial leadership in relationship to their subordinates.

Performance Appraisal and Personal Effectiveness

Confusion exists in the field of management because of what is commonly called performance appraisal. The use of the word 'performance' with regard to appraisal creates problems. Managers would generally prefer to have performance appraisal systems where there are objective indicators of output. In reality, people cannot be employed to produce designated outputs, since they cannot control the resources they are given or changing external circumstances.

People are employed to use their capability to do their best in producing the outputs that they are assigned. They should be paid for the level of capability they are able to use in working to achieve the output. For this reason the requisite process is called personal effectiveness appraisal rather than performance appraisal.

In an organization that is requisite Manager A holds Subordinate Manager B accountable for the results of the work and results of the working behavior of Subordinate C. C works to produce the output that B assigns in terms of quantity, quality and time within resources and policy. C is employed to use his/her applied capability in working to produce the outputs that B assigns. These capabilities include creativity and the use of discretion and exercise of judgment in decision-making. Manager A appraises the effectiveness of Manager B and Manager B appraises the effectiveness of C.

Purposes of the Personal Effectiveness Appraisal System

The purposes of personal effectiveness appraisals are to:

- let subordinates know how their manager judges their personal effectiveness
- provide an opportunity for subordinates to express their views and have a discussion with their manager about their personal effectiveness
- provide an opportunity for managers to coach their subordinates and develop action plans with them for improved performance
- provide input into compensation decisions

Applied Capability

Applied capability in doing work in order to produce outputs was discussed in Chapter Two. An understanding of applied capability is important in judging personal effectiveness. Applied Capability is a comprehensive concept. It is a function of a person's current potential capability, of his/her valuing the work, the degree of knowledge a person has that can be used in a skilled way and an absence of negative temperament.

The less interested individuals are in what they are doing, the less commitment they have to using their full capability. In order to use applied capability as fully as possible, it is necessary for a person to value the role s/he is occupying.

An employee may choose to work below their level of capability for any number of reasons. For example, a corporate librarian in a Stratum III role, who would be capable of working at Stratum V, instead uses her capability to run a successful community theater in her free time.

Negative temperament (-T) refers to the characteristics that inhibit someone's ability to carry out assigned work. Hence, (-T) can affect someone's applied capability.

In determining a subordinate's personal effectiveness, managers are given a system that allows them to state their judgments in terms of the level at which that person is working. They judge how much applied capability each subordinate is bringing to bear in doing his or her work, with 'work' defined as what one does in achieving a task or goal, not the actual output.

Appraisal as a Continuing Process

Personal effectiveness appraisal is not a once-a-year event. Managers and subordinates should have a continuing dialog in this regard throughout the year. In particular it is important for the manager to give the subordinate feedback whenever s/he has completed an important assignment. As part of this process, managers coach subordinates on a regular basis to help them become more effective in their roles.

The annual personal effectiveness appraisal acts as a summary of the coaching and personal effectiveness discussions held during the year. At this time targets for development in the subordinate's current role may be discussed and set for the coming year. This annual appraisal also provides input into the manager's decision about merit compensation for the subordinate.

Employees' Personal Effectiveness Accountabilities

Employees are accountable for using their skills, knowledge and experience in creative ways to work toward attainment of their assigned tasks. They are expected to use their full capability in working on the tasks they are given. Employees are accountable for clarifying their assignments with their manager, if necessary, and to let their manager know when they encounter problems that prevent them from achieving their goals.

The personal effectiveness appraisal system involves honest self-assessment on the part of the subordinate. This means identifying personal strengths as well as areas for improvement. Employees are expected to spend time and energy to take advantage of opportunities afforded by the company to develop the skills and knowledge necessary to grow in their present role.

Equilibration, the MoR's Role in Appraisal

As was mentioned in Chapter Three, in order for the personal effectiveness appraisal process to work properly, achieving consistency, fairness and balance, the MoR must review all of his/her immediate managers' judgments of the level of effectiveness of their subordinates. This process is called **equilibration**. It ensures that one manager is not placing everybody up at the top all the time while another tends to give subordinates lower judgments of effectiveness and smaller salary increases. The quality of managers' judgments does vary and it is the MoR's accountability to see that employees are treated in a reasonably even manner. The more requisite the system, the less variation will be found in these judgments.

It is the accountability of managers-once-removed to do an equilibration review, at least annually, in which s/he looks at the patterns in the appraisal process in each subordinate manager's group to ensure that they are all applying reasonably common standards.

MERIT REVIEW

In a requisite organization each employee is paid in accord with his/her level of applied capability as judged by his/her manager and is paid within a work band. Because a manager's complexity of information processing and the manager's role is one stratum higher than his/her subordinates, the essential conditions exist which enable a manager in a requisite organization to accurately judge personal effectiveness and to fine-tune individual pay.

The annual compensation review for an individual subordinate is part of the close working relationship between manager and subordinate in which the subordinate understands the discretion that the manager has with respect to judgments of his/her personal effectiveness.

If a manager is not coaching and providing regular feedback as to effectiveness, the subordinate can ask to have this done. If the manager is not fully carrying out these requisite Management Practices, the employee needs to ensure that his/her personal effectiveness is under review with the manager *during* the year and not a procedure that happens just once a year, causing the salary review to take place without a continuous and systematic background.

All too often organizations experience a period of several days devoted to rushed appraisals with no one getting any other work done. Then the process is forgotten for the next 12 months. Managers know they should talk with the immediate subordinates about their performance throughout the year, but in many organizations this does not happen. Requisite coaching and appraisal procedures require that personal effectiveness appraisal and coaching happen as a continuing, ongoing process.

SELECTION

Selection of someone to fill a vacant role occurs by having the Manager-once-Removed create a slate of candidates from which the immediate manager of the role chooses a preferred candidate. This screening procedure helps ensure long term stability, as well as continuing development, of the company pool of talent.

The immediate manager is not authorized to appoint someone to the vacant role if that individual does not fit the requirements of the role as established by the MoR. MoRs are not to try to get someone placed in a role whom the immediate manager feels cannot do the work of the role. Immediate managers do not have to take any candidate whom they deem unacceptable. This is one of the minimum authorities of all managers. It ensures that managers have as subordinates only those individuals whom they judge capable of doing the work in the roles they occupy.

The Selection Process

When a vacancy occurs, or a new role is established, the following procedure provides a process that ensures fairness and justice and enables the manager of the vacant role to select a competent new subordinate.

Specifying the Role

The first step in the selection process is to describe the requirements of the vacant role on a role specification form that includes:

- the level of work of the role which indicates the level of complexity of information processing required
- the type of role which gives an indication of the values needed for full commitment
- the major tasks in the role
- the skilled knowledge and any professional qualifications that are needed

Human Resources Recommends a Full Slate to the MoR

The second step is for Human Resources to prepare for the MoR a slate listing in alphabetical order everyone with the currently judged potential to work at the level of the role. These lists are blind with respect to gender, color, ethnicity, age and other bias. This list, for example, would include everyone judged to have mid-III potential for a mid-III role. If a wider slate is desired, the list could include everyone with low-, mid-, or high Stratum III potential.

This list should be prepared in three sections:

1. Those currently in roles one stratum or more below their potential who are being considered for a possible promotion.

2. Any individuals who have been over-promoted to roles above their potential and who would be in line for a role appropriate to their potential.

3. Employees with potential at the level of work of the role, who are in line for lateral transfers for career development.

Internal and External Candidates

An important policy with regard to fair treatment of current employees is that they are made aware of vacancies through the posting of certain roles as determined by policy. Vacancy notices should be circulated so that employees know about the vacancies and have the opportunity to apply to be considered for the slate being developed for the vacant role.

The organization has information on internal candidates with regard to judged potential capability, commitment and skilled knowledge. There is background information on their personal effectiveness from appraisals that are on file. The MoR knows many of the possible candidates from personal experience and the regular talent pool development meetings. This information is helpful in developing a slate of possible candidates from employees who are interested in, and capable of, the open position.

If external candidates are deemed desirable, these individuals can be initially screened by Human Resources and/or the MoR. The list of the best qualified internal, and if desired, external candidates is reduced to consist of those with the best qualifications.

MoR Develops Short List

Once this list is developed as described, the MoR develops a short list of individuals whom s/he judges able to fill the role requirements. In reducing the initial slate to a short list, the MoR will prepare an annotated list for discussion with the manager of the role so that his/her inputs can be taken into account.

The Immediate Manager Chooses from Short List

The immediate manager makes his/her selection from the short list. If the manager vetoes all the individuals on the short list, another short list must be prepared by the MoR. The hiring manager may exercise a veto only in terms of his/her judgment that an individual does not have the applied capability to do the work required.

INDUCTION

Induction is the process a manager uses to provide subordinates new to a role with the information necessary to do the work of that role. It is the immediate manager's accountability to let all new employees, or current employees who have been moved to a new role, know what is expected of them. Induction includes:

- a description of the role and the tasks assigned to it
- cross-functional accountability and authority
- current problems and priorities
- relevant policies and procedures
- reporting methods
- any other information that will help the employee gain a well-rounded knowledge of the role.

When an employee is new to the organization as well as the role, the manager can assign an experienced subordinate to introduce the newcomer to colleagues and significant people in other sections and help the newcomer learn about the organization. S/he should also tell the employee what it is like to work in the location, how to get around, how to get needed services and understand the customs, practices and conditions of employment.

Induction needs to take place in the first few weeks to a month. Managers are to see that employees at every level are fully introduced to their role. Sound induction helps someone new to the role quickly begin productive work. It also gives the new subordinate a reassuring sense of being in a reliable and trustworthy situation.

One organization that was implementing all requisite Management Practices found that by providing complete induction, mid level managers became fully productive within two months of assuming a new role, whereas formerly it took up to six months for this to happen.

DESELECTION AND DISMISSAL WITH CAUSE

There are circumstances when the manager has to initiate the removal of a subordinate from his/her role. For example, the manager may have made a bad selection or the role may be changing in such a way that the person cannot reasonably be expected to keep up. When a manager judges that a subordinate is not able to carry out the work that is required, s/he has the authority to request this person's removal from a role, but not removal from the employment by the company. Dismissal for cause is a very different matter. The need for dismissal with cause arises when someone grossly and blatantly breaks laws, rules and regulations or when dangerous situations occur because of an employee's negligence. Both deselection and dismissal actions need to be documented in accord with company policy and legal requirements.

Deselection

There is a requisite process for deselection when it is necessary because the person cannot do the work. The first step is to discussion the situation with the subordinate. If it is a case of not being able to keep up, the manager will point out where s/he judges that person's capability is unacceptable or describe to the person whatever non-performance the manager is experiencing. The subordinate in question has a chance to discuss the problem with the manager from his/her perspective. With this information in mind, the manager coaches the person and tries to help him/her improve.

If the unacceptable performance continues, the manager gives a warning and continues coaching in an effort to help the person perform successfully in that role. Throughout this process, the manager lets his/her own manager know about the situation. If there is still not sufficient improvement, the manager gives a second warning and provides continuing coaching. If the person feels unfairly treated s/he will have the opportunity to discuss it with the MoR. In this case the three people involved (the subordinate, the immediate manager and the MoR) meet to talk about the situation.

If the person continues to perform unacceptably after the discussions, the coaching and the warnings, the manager will request that the MoR, with the help of Human Resources, attempt to find alternative employment for this employee in the company. Sufficient time needs to be allowed for this to happen. If another place in the organization cannot be found, then the person will be released by HR on behalf of the company, with the same entitlements as someone let go as a result of downsizing. This is not a punitive situation.

Dismissal with Cause

Dismissal with cause occurs when an employee breaks the law, behaves outside generally acceptable norms or commits a major infraction of the policies and guidelines of the company such as theft, fighting on-site or dealing in drugs. The specifics for dismissal with cause are set by corporate policy. The immediate manager refers this type of dismissal to the MoR. Human Resources is involved to ensure adherence to local and federal policies.

MANAGERIAL MEETINGS

Managers at every level in the organization need to have regular meetings with their subordinates. All of a manager's immediate subordinates form the manager's team through which s/he gets the work of the unit done. Managers meet with their subordinate team to review priorities and changing conditions, problems and ideas for solutions and strategic considerations. These two-way discussions are essential for clear, continuing communication and context setting.

When decisions are required as part of a managerial meeting, it is the manager who makes the decision. Consensus, while useful, is not required. Decision making is not a group activity.

The manager meets on a regular basis with his/her full team of immediate subordinates. It is often useful for the manager to include all SoRs as well. Sometimes it is appropriate to meet with just one or more immediate subordinate managers and all of their subordinates, depending upon the issues. How frequently these various meetings are necessary depends upon circumstances. Many managers meet with their subordinate teams weekly and hold three-level meetings, including SoRs, quarterly or twice a year. One organization that was handling a critical turnaround held an audioconferencing meeting every morning involving all managers at Stratum IV and above in many locations. In rapidly changing fields such as brokerage daily meetings are quite common.

There are two major types of managerial meetings. The first is information sharing, the second is idea generation.

Information Sharing Meetings

In information sharing meetings the manager provides context for the work of the unit by talking about the issues at hand and why certain kinds of tasks have been assigned. Problems are dealt with that affect the unit, the manager and his/her subordinates in terms of their collaborative work. Information sharing portions of meetings provide an opportunity for the team of subordinates to see the big picture and also to discuss issues with the manager and with each other. Managers use information gained to make decisions in these meetings or at a later time.

Idea Generation Meetings

Managers work on idea generation in meetings with subordinates when they want to deal with a problem or problems they may not know how to tackle or where they would like to consider a variety of ideas. When doing this managers work together with some or all of their subordinates and encourage them to bring forward ideas in an open discussion, usually with no decision made at the time. A method sometimes used is called 'brain-storming' where ideas are set forth without critical analysis to encourage a wide range of thinking and creativity. Idea generation meetings are important because they provide a setting in which the group has an opportunity to work together, to test each other's ideas, and to learn about each other on a continuing basis.

Managerial Decision Making

Managers may make decisions in these meetings as a result of information that has come forward or s/he may make decisions at a later time. It is, of course, important to communicate these decisions.

CONTINUAL IMPROVEMENT

Continual improvement activities are essential to every organization. However, setting up a separate total quality (TQM) system with committees, councils, and quality circles undermines the work of the managerial system. Improvement activities should be in the hands of managers. Committees, councils and teams cannot do the work that managers can do. They cannot be held accountable as a group.

People are hired as individuals and can only be held accountable as individuals. It is managers who must be accountable for the improvement of the processes and systems that they are providing subordinates.

A manager cannot hold subordinates who are individual contributors accountable for the improvement of the processes that they have been given to work with, but managers can hold subordinate managers accountable to achieve improvement of the processes provided by that manager to his/her subordinates.

If subordinates see ways of improving processes, they are accountable to inform the manager. Managers also discuss possibilities with subordinates for getting the work done better. This two-way working enhances everyone's effectiveness and satisfaction.

Subordinates' personal growth, or their individual continual improvement, is their own personal concern. A manager can set up conditions for subordinates within which they can achieve personal growth, but the manager cannot hold any individual personally accountable for that growth. If a person chooses not to improve his/her ability to carry out a role, when s/he has the current potential capability to do so, the manager can discuss the consequences of this choice with the individual.

Steps in Continual Improvement

The steps necessary to get a solid continual improvement effort in an organization are to:

- hold managers accountable for the process
- maintain an ongoing analysis
- review and prioritize improvement projects
- provide assistance from staff specialists

Hold Managers Accountable for Continual Improvement

A continual improvement program cannot be set up as such. Continual improvement is not a program. What must be instilled throughout the managerial system is the idea that subordinates who are managers are held accountable by their managers not only for getting output through their subordinates, but also for continuously improving the processes that they control. These activities are an ordinary, ongoing part of their managerial leadership work and an important part of managerial accountability.

Maintain an Ongoing Analysis

Managers must maintain an ongoing analysis of the processes that they assign to their subordinates. This applies to work being done in all functions, all departments and at all levels. Managers need to ensure that their subordinates who are managers are paying attention to possibilities for overcoming problems where quality is suffering and not under good control.

Managers need also to ensure that, where possible, systematic, statistical methods of analysis are used. Every manager is held accountable for improving the systems within which s/he has subordinates working, since that is what the manager has control over.

Continual Improvement Priority List

Managers provide their subordinate managers with a list of items that they believe ought to be their priorities for projects oriented toward overcoming the most important blockages and shortcomings in the work processes. Both people keep this list under discussion and review it on a regular basis. As the managerial subordinates get the opportunity, they establish projects that allow them to tackle the topics that are at the top of the list. The manager holds his/her managerial subordinates accountable for always having at least one improvement project going on.

Staff Specialists Provide Assistance

Part of the regular work of staff specialists is to provide information and assistance to managers to enable continual improvement. For example, the HR specialists may inform managers about new legal requirements and help them revise procedures to conform to changes in the law.

Continual Improvement Project Teams

Setting up a special project team is one of the best methods for tackling a particular improvement that a manager wants to get under way. Improvement projects should be established in the same way that a manager would establish any ordinary task, that is, the manager gives a subordinate manager a QQT/R in assigning the project.

The managerial subordinate is to produce a particular result, i.e., an improvement in the process being worked on by the team, to a specified quality, on time, and with given resources. The managerial subordinate can either manage the quality project team directly or designate a team leader.

Continual Improvement on the Shop Floor

The people who are engaged in doing the work are in a very good position to understand the work process, to know where the difficulties are, and to come up with suggestions as to what ought to be done. On the shop floor this means getting the cooperation and collaboration of operators. It is not necessary to set up self-directed teams to do this. It is essential to set up clear and effective managerial accountability, where every operator has a real, first line manager and there is no one between the operators and their first line managers.

These first line managers are held accountable for maintaining a relationship with each one of their subordinates and for operating as fully accountable managers with regular meetings with subordinates and all other managerial duties.

In a union shop first line managers are accountable for understanding the company's agreements with the trade unions and for ensuring that they work explicitly and consistently within those agreements. These are binding agreements, and the company is accountable for ensuring that they are carried out. They constitute limits or parameters within which everyone works. With these requisite conditions in place first line managers can be held accountable for continual improvement by their managers, ensuring that work is being done effectively and, if there are problems, determining where improvement efforts should be focused.

Continuous Systems Improvement

In Japan in the late 1940s, Dr. W. Edwards Deming brought into focus both the statistical methods for achieving continuous reduction in process variance and the importance of attaining that reduction. Process variance reduction can be brought about by improving the methods themselves, by changing resources, and many other techniques. The aim is to move from a situation in which the control limits for processes are wide and to get those limits narrowed, so that these processes are controlled in such a way that the extent of variance is reduced. Japanese companies became excellent at continuing reduction of process variance, not just in manufacturing, but in all functions. This is the critical aim of the approach initiated and developed by Dr. Deming.

Dr. Deming taught the Japanese to introduce continuous improvement into the systems as they existed, that is, through the managerial system. He did this to ensure that first line managers were always working within quality limits, maintaining quality standards and producing their outputs just-in-time. Continual improvement is built into the managerial process: it is not a stand-alone undertaking.

America took note of Dr. Deming's work in the late 1970s. It was erroneously perceived in the U.S. that the success of Japan's continuous improvement efforts was the result of quality circles, committees and teams. However, it has always been in and through requisite managerial work that continuous improvement has been achieved in Japan. The quality circle team processes were introduced into Japanese industry in the early 1960s, a decade or more after the great changes in Japanese quality and just-in-time working had been attained.

A major contribution of Dr. Deming's work was the application of statistical methods to systematic process variance analysis. These methods have great advantage when used by managers. All managers should understand systematic, analytical approaches based on statistical analysis. Managers need to understand variance in the processes that they are controlling, ways of analyzing to find where priorities lie, where maximum gains can be achieved by getting those processes under increasingly effective control and getting variance operating within narrower and narrower limits. This understanding leads to substantial savings in direct cost, in the speed at which work can be done and in quality.

Continual Improvement at Every Level

Continual improvement is necessary throughout the organization. The corporate CEO at Stratum VII looks for continual improvement on major issues that affect the whole corporation. The Stratum V business unit president has improvement projects underway that apply to the processes governing work throughout the unit, and s/he considers and communicates where improvement priorities need to be placed throughout all of the functions. In order for improvement to go on throughout the corporation, senior managers must carry out their own accountabilities for ensuring that continuous improvement work goes on in their areas and that this accountability then cascades down through the organization.

Chapter 6

THE NOVUS STORY

In 1991 Mitsui & Co. Ltd. and Nippon Soda, Ltd. jointly acquired the Feed Ingredients Business from Monsanto Company. Dr. W. Joseph Privott, who was then running this business, was asked to become president of the new company. The new owners gave Dr. Privott the freedom to organize this new entity as he saw fit.

One of his early activities was to seek out ways of creating a work environment that would result in both business success and treatment of employees in a socially responsible way—providing a great place to work. As part of that effort, Dr. Privott attended a week-long seminar at the Levinson Institute. Dr. Elliott Jaques presented part of the seminar.

The ideas Dr. Jaques set forth appealed to Joe and he believed they would help him achieve his objectives for the new company. In particular, the logic and internal consistency of Requisite Organization concepts interested Joe Privott because they provided an approach to management as a science rather than an 'ad hoc' art. (Joe is a Ph.D. scientist as were many of the senior managers at Novus at that time.)

Joe Privott found in Elliott Jaques' ideas a practical approach that would help him not only enable Novus to achieve its mission and be financially successful but also to provide a healthy place to work. Joe asked Elliott who he would suggest to come to St. Louis to help implement the system, and Elliott suggested Nancy Lee, who had been working with his ideas for a number of years. Joe asked Nancy for a commitment of two weeks a month until the implementation of requisite concepts was well underway.

Thus began an almost ideal requisite project. Here was a newly formed company where the private owners gave the president the freedom to establish the philosophy and practices that he felt were most appropriate. One year from its founding the work started that would result in a nearly requisite organization.

Background on Monsanto and Novus

In the 1950's Monsanto, a St. Louis-based company, began applying chemistry to and developing businesses in three areas related to feeding the world: plant production, animal production and food production. It was soon recognized at Monsanto that the most significant payoff was in the area of herbicides for more efficient plant production. Monsanto, therefore, focused most of its resources in the plant area but maintained small businesses in animal and food production.

In the mid-1970's, Monsanto scientists made a major discovery that led to a new lower cost in the production of methionine, a nutritional animal feed additive. In the early 80's Monsanto built the world's largest methionine plant and began to grow market share. Joe Privott was brought in as the plant was being built to develop and execute the marketing plan.

By 1990 Monsanto again decided its strategy would be to focus most of its efforts on crop chemicals with an emphasis on biotechnology. The company also decided to divest the Feed Ingredients business which had methionine as its major product.

During the new company's formation it acquired a name which, under the circumstances, was very appropriate. One of the employees suggested that the company be named Novus, a Latin word which roughly translates as 'new beginning', and this name was adopted.

In the early years, Novus' mission was 'help meet the growing worldwide demand for high quality, affordable food'. There were 160 employees and gross sales were about $250 million dollars.

A New Beginning using Requisite Principles and Practices

Early steps in the introduction of requisite organization included:

- educating the senior management team of nine individuals
- analyzing the extant organization
- getting preliminary judgments of the complexity of information processing of each person in the top three levels.

Educating Senior Management

The senior management team was introduced to requisite concepts as part of their regular weekly management meetings. These meetings were extended to allow a one hour presentation on a particular aspect of RO followed by a question and answer period. These presentations by Joe and Nancy were intended to both educate these managers and gain their agreement as to the reasonableness and usefulness of these concepts. Nancy also prepared a brief written paper on each key concept for use in these meetings.

Novus was fortunate to have Sir Roderick Carnegie visit early in the project when he made a presentation on requisite concepts and his experience with them as CEO of CRA, an Australian mining company. His question and answer period helped the senior management explore their doubts about requisite procedures. Rod had worked for more than a decade with Elliott in the formation of many requisite concepts. Rod's visit brought a great deal of credibility to the Requisite Organization approach and also provided encouragement to senior management to spend the necessary time and energy to implement the system.

Analyzing the Extant Organization

Nancy undertook a review of the extant organization, that is the organization as it existed in terms of roles, reporting relationships, work being done and time span of key tasks in each role. She interviewed Joe first as to the work he was expecting of each the management team's units.

Next she interviewed each member of the management team as to their understanding of the results that were expected from their units. She then explored how they divided this work up among subordinate roles. At the same time she sought data on some of the longest tasks for which they believed they were responsible, as well as information on the longer tasks they delegated to subordinate roles. Occasionally Joe's view and the understanding of a given manager were not fully aligned. When this was the case, Nancy worked to achieve full clarity and agreement.

This information yielded a picture of a Stratum VI organization comprised of five layers where virtually all the roles were Stratum II to Stratum VI. There were very few roles at Stratum I.

Stratum VI Organizations

At that point in time, the early 1990s, Elliott felt that a Stratum VI company was perhaps somewhat unstable and needed to grow to a Stratum VII or become a Stratum V organization. This had been his observation up until that time, although he was not able to articulate fully his reasons for the possible instability of Stratum VI companies. (Subsequently he came to believe that Stratum VI companies were viable as he experienced more and more of them, possibly occurring because they actually had only five layers, with most Stratum I work being handled by technology.)

In fact, Joe was interested in growing what had been a Stratum V business group within Monsanto, into a Stratum VII company that dealt with a wide variety of related products. He sought to have these products added largely through acquisition, but internal development and joint ventures were other possible avenues.

Initial Judgments of Employees' Complexity of Information Processing

Joe provided initial judgments of the Complexity of Information Processing (CIP) of each of his subordinates and Subordinates-once-Removed. (Joe's judgments over a number of years were recorded. Not surprisingly the changes in the judgments paralleled the expected growth in complexity of individuals as anticipated on the Potential Progress Chart developed by Dr. Jaques.)

The senior management team also judged the complexity of information processing of their subordinates and Subordinates-once-Removed. This gave a picture of the capability of the employees from Stratum VI to Stratum III.

Joe felt Elliott's approach to judging complexity of information processing clarified the issue of capability and separated it from values, knowledge and temperament. Requisite Organization provided concepts, a vocabulary and tools to consider these quite different issues and to talk about them.

Addressing Issues of Temperament

As the power of the use of requisite practices began to become evident at Novus, Joe turned his attention to issues of temperament. He wanted a method of understanding and discussing issues of behavior and a way to take temperament into consideration in staffing decisions. His goal was to find a way to assist individuals and groups to behave more effectively at work.

Nancy recommended Ken Wright, a specialist in this area, who also has a deep understanding of Requisite Organization. Ken used the Human Synergistics' instrument as an information gathering tool and catalyst both for individual discussions and to enhance understanding of interpersonal issues within groups and teams. Work in this area began along with the ongoing implementation of requisite practices.

Examining Cross-Functional Working Relationships

Another area that was addressed early in the project was that of the interface between units. An off-site meeting was held, to review areas where improving clarity in accountability and authority between roles reporting to different managers would likely produce increased effectiveness for Novus. The requisite descriptions of Task Initiating Role Relationships (TIRRs) were used as the means of addressing some of these issues and specifying what the roles involved needed to do. Joe was aware that this was often a source of interpersonal problems that were apt to lessen when the relationship between roles in different areas were clearly described.

In practice it was found that not all of the TIRRs were needed and a smaller subset was developed for ongoing work in this area. These relationships were renamed Cross Activity Relationships (CARs) to indicate that not all of the requisite concepts were included.

Developing Requisite Processes for Novus

Working with the Manager of Human Resources, Sabrena Hamilton, a document was developed to clearly state Key Accountabilities. This document coordinated with an appraisal document that was designed at the same time and that was intended to be used informally at mid-year and for the formal annual appraisal.

A manual was developed for all Novus managers that described the integrated process of identifying and communicating to each employee their key accountabilities, providing feedback and coaching when tasks were completed and judging overall personal effectiveness. These processes plus the other eight requisite managerial leadership practices were described in the manual. The full set of procedures, as well as the manual, was entitled The Novus Management System (NMS). Sabrena and Nancy also reviewed all Novus policy documents to modify any aspects of policy and procedures that were non-requisite.

Key Accountabilities Document (KAD)

This document was designed to include key tasks and general responsibilities, team assignments and critical cross-functional accountability and authority. A general statement was included to the effect that persons in managerial roles will also be judged with regard to their full use of the requisite managerial leadership practices. (Novus' document is similar in design to the Role Specification form recommended as Requisite.)

Personal Effectiveness Appraisal (PEA)

One of the areas of extensive discussion in designing the Personal Effectiveness Appraisal process and the document was whether or not to include 'exceeds expectations' as well as 'meets expectations', 'below expectations' and 'unacceptable'. The decision was made to follow Elliott's recommendation of not including an 'exceeds' rating, since meeting expectations is what is expected of all employees.

Joe Privott found that an important contribution made by requisite concepts was that accountabilities should be identified by the manager's intended time to completion. This might well be shorter or longer than the annual appraisal cycle. When it was necessary to judge tasks lasting more than a year for the annual review, managers were given the option of considering the setting of a milestone in the progress of that task.

Educating Employees about the Novus Management System

With the KAD and PEA and the Novus Management System (NMS) manual ready for use, each member of the senior management team set up an educational session for all of their subordinates. Nancy assisted in these programs which were held not only in St. Louis but around the world as part of regional meetings.

Novus has many Stratum II individual contributors and it quickly became apparent that a shorter version of the manual was needed to educate them from their perspective with regard to the Novus Management System and to communicate expectations of the accountability and authority of all Novus employees. This version of the NMS was prepared and also used as part of the educational program.

These programs were completed throughout the world over a period of about three months.

Other Requisite Practices

As the second year of requisite implementation began with the task assignment and appraisal processes in place and the initial education completed, attention turned to other requisite practices such as selection and orientation. Nancy and Sabrena wrote a manual to aid managers throughout the world in applying requisite principles in interviewing and selecting employees. An orientation program was designed and provided to newly hired employees.

Level of Work and Organization Structure

Issues of organization structure and the level of work in each role had been reviewed during the first year of the implementation. Principles used here were provided as part of the educational process. Some changes had been made where, for example, a role incumbent was found to be not of the level of complexity of information processing required by the work of the role. But it was not until this point that a decision could be made in determining how level of work was to be used in Novus.

It was decided by Joe to use two, rather than three bands, within Strata I, II and III and have only one band in the higher Strata. Novus roles were placed in these bands using a combination of time span measurement and executive judgment as to what would be required in the future. Roles were calibrated across the organization with all senior staff working together. Over time, the staff was gradually deployed requisitely, based on judgment of complexity of information processing and the other aspects of suitability for a role, which are values and skilled knowledge.

Compensation

After two years of work resulting in Novus being organized requisitely in terms of roles and role incumbents, it then became possible to turn attention to the compensation system. It is only when an organization is requisitely structured and staffed and requisite managerial leadership practices are in place, that it is possible to implement requisite compensation.

Sabrena Hamilton was a specialist in compensation and had many years of experience in traditional compensation, especially with regard to its application in a global company. She asked several compensation specialist organizations to assist her in using requisite compensation, but none were able to integrate requisite concepts into their existing methodologies.

> "So, I had a number of conversations with Thad Simons, corporate counsel, and Nancy on this topic and then shut myself in a room for two days to fully understand the implication of using 'X' and pay differential based on level of work of a role, as the basis of total compensation. I made some initial calculations as to what this would look like in some of the many countries around the world where we have employees.

"It became apparent to Thad and me that since we had uniformly defined complexity of roles worldwide we could benchmark pay at each level and then adjust as needed to the realities of various labor markets. We separated pay increases from structure movements. Our calculations included all aspects of compensation such as benefits, which tend to vary widely between countries plus the annual and the long-term incentive plans. While we will never have a totally requisite compensation system since we have incentive pay for all employees, we were nonetheless able to apply most of the principles successfully. And we found that once you understand and apply the basics of requisite compensation, you don't need compensation specialists to keep the system going."

Talent Pool Development

In addition to being corporate counsel, Thad Simons was also the head of new business development and human resources. Working with Sabrena and Nancy, he set up a requisite talent pool process beginning in year two. The senior management team met several times a year to review all roles that needed to be filled in the next several years and all employees who had the CIP required by these roles.

Discussions focused on each employee with regard to their qualifications in terms of what they valued in the work environment; their education, experience and skilled knowledge. A major outcome was to share information as to each employee's CIP as agreed by their manager and MoR and get additional information on each person.

A form was developed that captured information in terms of who was considered:

- ready in the areas of CIP or when they might be ready
- whether they valued the role in question (or what steps should be taken to explore that further)
- whether or not they had the necessary skilled knowledge (or what needed to be taken to develop it and plans for that to happen)

Talent Pool meetings were regularly scheduled to repeat this process. In addition, all employees who were judged capable of working at level 3 (middle management roles) or higher were reviewed by the group to calibrate judgments between the senior manager and Joe and to review and add to the pool of talent on a continuing basis.

The senior management team commented on how constructive this approach was compared to earlier experiences some of them had had where issues of personality were largely the focus of attention.

Embedding the Novus Management System

Also starting in the second year, Joe Privott instituted an annual review of the full Novus Management System at the annual meeting of employees in St. Louis. He conducted this review personally, sending a clear message of the importance of these practices and ensuring that all employees were familiar with the requisite practices contained in the NMS.

These annual education sessions consisted of three parts: one was Joe Privott's review of the NMS; the second was a review of Human Synergistics to continue to enhance personal understanding of behavior in the business setting and interpersonal cooperation; and the third was the presentation of a number of workshops on other management skills such as giving feedback, coaching, communicating clearly, making effective presentations and dealing with cross cultural issues. Much of the material was developed by Nancy and all of the material was consistent with requisite principles.

Joe also participated in all new employee orientation sessions giving the segment on the NMS, demonstrating his commitment to it. He also used each issue of the Novus newsletter to address some aspect of the NMS.

He ended these articles and the educational sessions by asking employees "to hold him accountable for following the System" and stating that he would "hold them accountable for doing so as well."

Thoughts about the Novus Project

Joe Privott retired from Novus in 1999 and subsequently became a consultant to corporate presidents, helping them understand and implement Requisite Organization. Following are some of his thoughts about his experience of bringing these concepts into Novus.

"During the years of implementing requisite ideas we learned a lot that helped us. One of the things that appealed to me initially about Elliott's ideas is that it gave us tools to make clearer judgments about individuals. We all make those judgments but with requisite concepts and language, we had a sophisticated mental model of what we were doing which gave us more confidence in our judgments of individuals. There is a tendency to want to quantify performance but one needs to make a judgment about whether each person was operating at full capability under the prevailing circumstances. This can't be measured; it has to be judged. Elliott's concepts gave us a frame of reference for making and reviewing these judgments of employees' effectiveness under prevailing circumstances."

"The concepts embodied in 'capability' and 'level of work of a role' were especially helpful in understanding situations where individuals, who had been capable of their roles, seemed no longer effective as the organization and the work grew in complexity. This problem is common in successful and growing organizations and is a very difficult one to deal with. Understanding its causes is a giant step toward deciding how to resolve the problem while valuing the worth and dignity of the individual involved."

"The talent pool process we developed using requisite concepts helped us to think about the organization we needed in the future in terms of roles and the level of work that would be involved. We had a common language to do an assessment of our current talent pool and analyze our current staff in terms of their complexity of information processing (CIP), their values and knowledge, skill and experience. We then had a sound basis to provide development plans for specific individuals that we wanted to prepare for future roles."

"Temperamental issues were handled by Ken Wright's work which helped key employees to see themselves with objectivity and how their behavior at work affects others. One of my key employees told me that he couldn't stop himself from having his first thoughts about ideas be negative ones, but he could control what he did with those thoughts. He said that once he realized the impact of this behavior on others, he learned to stop himself from making cynical, put-down remarks that cut off creative discussions."

"As one involved in Novus from its inception, I had a passion to drive the company forward successfully. Using requisite principles gave me additional courage and confidence to develop my vision for the company and implement it. Along the way there were some events that were particularly significant in our ability to use and embed requisite concepts. One was the opportunity to discuss issues directly with Elliott in addressing problems. He was always available to Nancy and me by telephone and visited us in St. Louis on several occasions. He is sorely missed."

"Another was the day Rod Carnegie, former CEO of CRA, spent with us. Bringing in someone who had fully experienced requisite implementation and who had personally wrestled with the issues that arise while doing so, was a very important event giving me confidence and courage to continue to push forward in getting buy-in from my senior team and in enabling us to continue to move ahead."

"The combination of an understanding of differences in the complexity of information processing (CIP), with an understanding of temperaments and resulting behavioral patterns, was a powerful thing for me. It gave me a 'scientific basis' for designing the organization, assigning staff to roles and diagnosing performance shortfalls. Ultimately it gave me a basis for deciding on appropriate corrective actions. These were usually making reassignments to get a requisite role/CIP relationship, but occasionally it was coaching to help an employee manage a potentially dysfunctional temperament so as not to exhibit dysfunctional behavior. What I also found was that employees are better able to manage their potentially dysfunctional temperaments when they are assigned to roles with a level of complexity that matches their level of mental processing capability."

Joe's comments on the results of implementing RO, in conjunction with a focus on temperament, are that:

"Excellent business results were achieved (in both growth and profitability) compared to competitors and a healthy, constructive place to work was established. What started as a small unit in Monsanto that had 3% share of the domestic market grew to have 35% share of a world market that was itself growing at 6% and 10% annually. Using requisite principles contributed substantially to our success over the years and enabled me to deal openly, fairly and honestly with my employees."

Novus in the 21st Century

With Thad Simons as president of Novus, the corporate vision has evolved and it is now to 'help feed the world affordable, wholesome food' and Novus' goal is to 'build a self-renewing multi-product company'. Novus does business in 83 countries.

Requisite practices, embodied in the Novus Management System, continue in place and are well embedded in the culture. Attention to setting clear goals and enhancing individual effectiveness, has enabled Novus in four years to improve efficiency from about $1.5 million in sales per full time employee to more than $2.5 million today. The clarity, logic and consistency of requisite organization principles provide a substantial foundation for guiding and integrating the work of employees who are located in 24 countries. With sales approaching $500 million and a continuing strong growth rate of more than 10% per annum, Novus today is an outstanding example of a successful global organization that has implemented requisite principles and practices.

Chapter 7

THE ROCHE CANADA STORY

By *Charlotte Bygrave*
Formerly Senior Vice President, Human Resources

Background

The pharmaceutical industry has long been one of the world's most complex. In the early 1990's that complexity began accelerating at a spectacular rate.

F. Hoffmann-La Roche, Ltd., one of the leading global, research-oriented health care companies, realized that this rapidly accelerating complexity meant 'business as usual was no longer an option'. The industry's critical issues were growing in intensity—patent expirations, price pressures, drug development challenges, and regulatory and political pressures.

'Roche' responded to these issues with mergers and acquisitions, improved manufacturing processes, licensing-in of new drugs, and strategic alliances. They articulated other new directions, including managers acting as coaches and mentors, not commanders and controllers, the elimination of 'turfs' and organization silos, and the building of a stronger goal and process orientation.

In 1995 the senior management of the Canadian affiliate of the company, Roche Canada, asked Elliott Jaques and Nancy Lee to help them build an organization that could meet the demands and expectations of their corporate parent and achieve success, short and long term, in this unprecedented business environment.

The following highlights the work the Canadian senior management began with Elliott and Nancy to:

- establish an optimal organization structure;
- clarify accountabilities and authorities and cross-functional working relationships;
- develop the talent and capability of employees;
- establish high performance project teams;
- and implement the best managerial leadership practices to strengthen organizational governance, performance and success.

Roche Canada Prepares for the 21st Century

Early in 1993 the president and CEO of Roche Canada, Donald B. Brown, and his management team held an off-site meeting to identify responses to company and industry issues that would provide the highest value 'payoffs' to move the Canadian operation forward.

We considered several of the latest and best management practices—re-engineering, total quality management, and leadership training and development. However, we eventually decided that while these approaches were sound, they would be fragmented, partial solutions to what we sensed were far more fundamental and systemic issues. We needed to find an approach that would help us better define our issues and provide long lasting solutions.

A few months after the meeting, I attended one of Elliott's workshops on the Requisite Organization principles and practices. He presented a science of organization and management, clearly defined concepts about the underlying structure of the organization—its parts and properties and the relations between them. He explained that many organizational issues, widely diverse in appearance, were often just dissimilar forms of the same thing or had the same root causes. Many of the problems of organization and management were problems with the systems we used and not actually problems with the people.

I began to think that perhaps this was an approach the Roche Canada management team would find useful. It could help address issues such as:

- retaining talent;
- creating a learning organization;
- eliminating 'turfs' and functional silos affecting individual and organizational performance;
- helping managers get better at managing people;
- realizing the anticipated benefits of mergers;
- and improving the execution of our plans.

I presented the Requisite Organization approach to Don Brown, and he quickly saw it as a set of comprehensive, logical and integrated principles and practices that could help us structure and manage the organization for success. After learning about the principles and how to apply them in a three-day intensive workshop led by Nancy Lee and Kathryn Cason, the senior management group unanimously agreed that these principles represented the way they wanted to manage the people and the business. Moving ahead to implement the principles was delayed, however, due to other business issues.

About six months later, after a major acquisition (Syntex Corporation) and under the direction of a new president and CEO, Vic Ackermann, the senior managers wanted to know 'what had happened with those principles' and felt we needed them more after the acquisition than we did before it. Perhaps the principles could help us better manage the challenges of integrating two organizations.

I was asked to take on the role of internal project manager and work with Elliott Jaques and Nancy Lee to develop a plan for optimizing the organization structure needed as a result of the acquisition. We expected that with the right or requisite structure we'd have a critical part of what was needed to achieve the anticipated benefits of the acquisition and long term success.

Organizing To Deliver Roche Strategy

Working with Elliott and Nancy, the management team learned exactly what organization structure was and why it was so essential to developing and executing strategy while providing a socially healthy organization.

Vertical Organization Alignment

First, Elliott's time span concept and definitions of levels of complexity of work were applied to help the management group answer that most vexing question of how many working levels or layers the new organization should have.

Elliott interviewed the president and CEO to discuss his mandate and what he hoped to achieve. Together they discovered the level of complexity of work in his role and the boundaries of the top organization level. Next they discussed what Vic expected from each of his vice presidents to determine the complexity of work and organizational level of these roles. Nancy Lee and I interviewed managers below the vice president level and measured the time span for all other roles throughout the organization.

The time span concept reflected Elliott's 50 years of research which showed that the more complex the work, the further out in time it extends, and the greater the capability required to do the work. It was the task in a role with the longest targeted completion time that determined the complexity of work in the role and the capability required to do the work.

With time span we determined just the right number of organization levels we needed, defined the unique complexity of work to be done at each level and placed each role at the right level.

We established how far into the future were the longest tasks that each manager assigned to each of the roles in the organization. There was a high correlation between this time span method and our job evaluation system in measuring role complexity, but time span proved to be more effective and efficient. We were now using a single clear concept for measuring work complexity, and it enabled us to place roles at just the right organization level. It was definitely value added to our job evaluation system.

Using time span we were able to delve deeper into the meaning of work complexity and descriptions of its nature at each organization level. We learned that work complexity changes state from level to level and that the type of information processing or 'mental horsepower' required to do the work at each level was different.

One of the most fundamental concepts of the Requisite Organization approach is that levels (called strata in requisite work) in an organization are a reflection of levels of human capability, and the alignment of that capability and the complexity of work would be a prerequisite for success in the challenging environment in which the company was operating. Unless we got this alignment right, sustainable organization growth and development would be greatly constrained.

The information that Elliott, Nancy and I gathered showed that Roche had the right number of organization levels. However, the challenge would be ensuring that the capability of employees filling each role was at least equal to the complexity of the work in the role.

Along with my directors of human resources, I became well versed in applying the time span method so that we could support the management team in establishing and maintaining the right number of vertical levels and the role complexity required to do the work of the new organization.

Functional Organization Alignment

The management team next examined the somewhat top heavy and fragmented, functional structure resulting from the recent merger.

We decided on the best grouping of core business functions or mainstream operational and support functions (Sales, Marketing, Regulatory Affairs, Clinical Research, etc.) to sustain focus on customers, markets, competitive shifts, and other significant changes in the external environment. We developed clear definitions of accountabilities and authorities within and across functions.

The changes in the organization's vertical and functional alignment set the foundation for carrying out the long term strategic, operational and tactical, as well as the day to day, work of the organization.

Establishing Better Cross-Functional Working Relationships

Elliott, Nancy and I held workshops with each function to identify cross-functional working relationships negatively impacting the quality and speed of work done across functions. Managers identified issues related to cross-functional accountabilities, authorities and role relationships. We assisted the accountable managers, the first manager that had accountability for all of the relevant functions, in resolving issues in a way that made good business sense, and improved individual and departmental working relationships.

For example, the Marketing, Regulatory Affairs, and Clinical Research functions were able to work more efficiently together after the president clarified the accountability and authority that he wanted the vice presidents of each function to have with respect to the development of marketing materials. He assigned to Regulatory Affairs, the group accountable for securing government approval to market drugs, monitoring and auditing authority for all materials with respect to their scientific and medical accuracy. The Clinical Research function had the accountability and authority to provide input/advice to Regulatory Affairs. The Marketing function retained accountability and authority for the final production of medically and scientifically accurate marketing materials.

Managers learned the importance of clarifying cross-functional accountabilities and authorities, establishing conflict resolution mechanisms and setting context for conflict resolution by their direct reports working across functions.

Organization silos and the lack of collaborative efforts thought to be due primarily to negative 'politics' and 'personality conflicts' were lessened due to greater clarity of accountabilities and authorities between roles and functions. These clear cross-functional accountabilities and authorities replaced the vague or ill-defined integration mechanisms often used by organizations such as 'matrix organizations', 'dotted-line relationships', 'liaison task forces', 'sponsors and champions' and committees.

Clarifying the cross-functional role relationships allowed people to get on with their work in a more effective way, reducing conflict and inefficiencies and releasing employee energy, initiative and creativity.

The HR team and I found ourselves busy helping managers prepare new role descriptions to clarify and communicate cross-functional accountabilities and authorities that would facilitate more collaborative work among individuals and functions.

Establishing High-Performance Product Development and Launch Teams

With the optimal vertical and functional alignment of the organization established and clear accountabilities and authorities defined, we had a new framework for analyzing and resolving various problems, including those experienced by the product launch teams.

It had become apparent that the Canadian product development and launch teams were not functioning as well as anyone had expected.

Vic had established six or seven of these cross-functional teams and had assigned accountability and authority for the teams to the Executive Committee. He had experience working with these types of teams and knew their value to the timely launch of new products. A few weeks delay in launching a new product could cost the organization millions of dollars.

The teams were producing good outputs and results but they were 'leaping high hurdles' and 'running obstacle courses' to do so. The director of New Product Development and internal coach for the teams asked me for assistance in reviewing the teams' issues. She and I agreed to bring in an external consultant to help the teams identify their issues. With the help of this consultant the team identified their issues, but the team leaders decided that they were unable to find resolutions to their problems.

They needed the help of senior management and requested time on the agenda of an Executive Committee meeting to present their issues:

- They were quite pleased to be team leaders. However, several members of the committee were assigning tasks to them and this workload, along with that assigned by their 'home base' managers, was no longer bearable and soon it would be impossible for them to continue performing well. Frankly, they had too many 'bosses to please'. Could the Executive Committee help them resolve this problem?
- The 'home base' or functional managers still expected completion to standards of 100% of the 'regular' work they assigned to their direct reports who were on the teams. Who would decide the work priorities? Who would help the team members 'mend' the deteriorating work relationship with their 'real' or 'regular' managers?

- Team members had concerns with performance appraisals and compensation for the 'two jobs' they were performing. What effect should their team work have on their annual overall performance appraisal and compensation awards? Who would appraise their 'team work' and decide on rewards and recognition?
- Team leaders and members were having difficulty fielding questions from their peers regarding how one got chosen to be on a team and especially appointed team leader. Employees knew selection criteria had not been established and concluded the decisions were 'political'.
- There were other conflicts to be dealt with. Who would help resolve problems within the teams or between the teams and other functions and departments after team leaders had exhausted their best influencing and persuasive skills—to no avail? What accountability and authority did team leaders and members have anyway? How were team leaders and the team's consultant to solve problems such as members' non-attendance at important team meetings or a member's sub-optimal performance? Who could initiate the removal of a team member from the team when removal was warranted? How should the teams and the functional departments interact? Were the 'home base' or functional department managers in any way accountable for the teams' success and performance?

On hearing the complaints, the Executive Committee was somewhat shocked. They had no idea of the extent of the teams' problems. They considered a number of solutions, including giving the teams a 'break', controlling the flow of work to teams through one identified committee member, more 'technical' training for the teams, and, of course, granting much deserved rewards for the team members.

While these measure were somewhat helpful they did not address the root causes of the teams' issues, which we learned were organization structure issues such as lack of clear role relationships (accountabilities and authorities) between the teams and the functional departments (Marketing, Regulatory, Clinical Research); appointment of an accountable manager/executive for the teams; effective selection criteria for team members and leaders; and effective conflict resolution mechanisms.

How to structure and manage six or seven critical teams—the number growing due to several new products in the pipeline—was an organization design problem which even brought a 'furrowed brow' to Elliott's face. A small senior management task force was formed with Elliott as the external consultant and me as the internal advisor to review the issues. Elliott advised us that our product launches required two very different types of teams, project and coordinative teams. We would also need to know how to transition from project teams, needed to analyze and recommend a product's inclusion in the portfolio, to coordinative teams, which were needed to plan and execute the development and launch phases of the product launch process.

We analyzed and resolved the teams' issues using Requisite Organization design principles and practices. We developed:

- the accountabilities and authorities of team leaders and members for both project and coordinative teams;
- clearly defined role relationships between teams and the rest of the organization;
- selection criteria and processes for team leaders and members;
- processes for delegation of authorities; and
- guidelines for applying human resource management policies— personal effectiveness appraisals, rewards and recognition, training and development, and other types of team support.

Guidelines for establishing and maintaining the teams were reviewed, revised and documented. The new team design and infrastructure embedded in a well designed larger organization reduced team frustration, increased morale and enabled the teams to get on with their work, including moving down the path to reducing launch times.

Celebrations were held and rewards and recognition granted. Elliott's principles were turning out to be useful and practical 'stuff'.

Assessing the Talent Pool and Communicating the Results

Roche, as with all organizations, had increasing concerns about talent retention. A well-designed organization structure would be meaningless if the company could not retain and develop good talent.

A talent pool assessment process was developed to determine the strength of the current and future talent pool and the requirements for training and development, recruitment, and succession planning.

The process cascaded down from the top to the entry level of the organization. Elliott, Nancy and I held discussions with immediate managers and their managers about the capability of each of the individuals on their teams. It was a clean and efficient process. Unlike previous methods which asked managers to rate employees on several different skills, behaviors, traits and factors indicating capability, this process had one central question or focus—at which organization level did the individual have the capability to do work now, if they could get the necessary training and experience and if the role was one which the individual valued doing?

Elliott and Nancy prepared and previewed with me a 'wall-sized' progression chart showing all the data collected in our discussions, the organization level at which each individual could work today, his/her judged capability level, and predictions about how that capability would mature over time.

I led a meeting of the Executive Committee to review and discuss the talent pool information displayed on the progression chart. The entire talent pool was displayed and the committee could determine whether or not the organization had the current and future talent needed. The committee also reviewed the information for employee development and succession planning, and information to help managers and their managers develop and sustain an effective team of people. As the discussion progressed, changes were made to some assessments to achieve the highest levels of fairness and accuracy of assessments.

We decided on a pilot test to communicate the assessment results to 50 randomly selected employees (stratified sampling). The pilot test results showed that these employees felt that the new system produced simpler and fairer assessments: simpler, because employees and managers were using the same language and concepts about capability and considering one major factor; fairer, because of multiple inputs, including the employees' own input. They especially liked knowing assessments would be reviewed on an annual basis. The judgments were not 'once and for all' judgments, but could be changed as significant and additional information about an employee's capability was revealed through the completion of task assignments or other accomplishments.

The pilot results showed that 49 of the 50 employees agreed with the assessments and all 50 commented that they felt the process was an excellent one. Our policy was that disagreements about assessments were noted and marked for review and resolution at a later time when more information was available.

While the immediate manager provided input to the assessment of a direct report and helped him/her prepare for talent pool discussions, it was the immediate manager's manager, the Manager-once-Removed, who made the decision about an employee's capability and who was accountable for helping that employee understand how his/her capability could best be developed in the context of the company's business requirements.

Roche Canada could see that, long term, effective management of the new system would allow for more accurate forecasting and planning of human resources, better training and career development programs and more appropriate and respectful treatment for all employees.

Managerial Leadership Training

Creating and presenting managerial leadership training programs was another important part of the Requisite Organization approach at 'Roche'.

Having the required capability was a necessary but not sufficient condition for effective management—managers needed to be trained and held accountable for specific managerial practices. The training placed emphasis on management practices, not on 'management styles'. As long as a manager's behaviors were within the limits or bounds clearly articulated by the company, we learned to leave their personalities alone.

Nancy Lee, my staff and I provided all managers with opportunities to understand the managerial practices and the minimum authorities they needed to lead effectively and earn the trust of their direct reports.

Through roles plays and discussions each practiced:

- selecting new employees;
- training and coaching;
- conducting two way planning meetings;
- setting context, direction and prescribed limits;
- defining tasks;
- appraising performance;
- conducting merit reviews;
- and initiating the removal of a direct report from a role.

Managers-once-Removed learned they were accountable for: setting context and direction for the work of the two levels below them; integrating cross-functional work flows; human resource planning and development; and making sure that their immediate managers exercised effective managerial leadership practices and treated their direct reports equitably and with respect.

These practices became the backbone of the company's management training for all management levels. Our human resource management system and policies had been modified where necessary to be consistent with this training; that is, policies and procedures related to recruitment, interviewing and hiring, personal effectiveness appraisal, career planning and advancement, and reward and recognition.

The training and development of Roche managers would ensure that managers were using consistent management practices, in line with the organization's values, to secure the willing commitment and best endeavors of their direct reports. This would enable achievement of the organization's desired outcomes and results, better employee morale and improved governance. Even our senior managers said they enjoyed the training and found it beneficial.

Requisite Rewards and Recognition

There were changes to other important policies and practices at Roche. We took an approach to rewards and recognition that was far 'outside the box' and that eliminated predictive criteria-based bonus schemes.

The nature of work is complex, and employees must face and overcome unpredictable and unanticipated obstacles on their way to achieving a task/goal. This unpredictability, inherent especially in the complex work in the higher level roles, renders predictive criteria-based pay systems somewhat ineffective. These systems make no allowance for actual performance conditions that vary significantly from the predicted conditions; rather, they focus and reward employees for achieving or coming close to achieving a certain level of results or outcomes, usually quantitative. This directs employees to focus on how to achieve the numbers, which could require behaviors not consistent with doing the right thing given the circumstances. Also, one employee might accomplish more complex and higher quality work under more difficult circumstances but with lower quantitative results and might therefore receive a lower bonus than another, whose less complex work under less difficult circumstances generated higher quantitative results and therefore a larger bonus—for example, the inevitable 'windfalls' in sales.

As a result, bonus programs sometimes caused poor morale, precipitated employee behaviors outside of acceptable standards, and created poor relationships between management and employees. Employees would often ask "what does the bonus, compared to base pay, reward or pay me for? Does it mean the company does not expect my full commitment and best performance for the base pay I receive?" These were difficult questions to answer.

Each of the three Roche Canada business divisions had the authority, however, to decide what they felt was best for their business—to retain or eliminate bonus pay schemes. They decided to roll incentive pay into base salary. Two divisions retained incentives as a small part of total compensation for the Sales and Marketing staff.

Special awards, reviewed by the appropriate manager and the human resources department to ensure consistency of treatment, could still be granted to any employee for exceptional performance. These cases were determined after the fact—that is, at the end of the performance period.

There was a great deal of work for the human resources department in reviewing the impact of this change on salary driven benefits programs and particularly on the defined benefit pension plan. It was a change affordable by the company.

The entire compensation program was reviewed to ensure pay ranges were linked to organization levels and levels of complexity of work. Clearly defined role accountabilities and alignment of work complexity with organization levels reduced concerns about lack of equity and fairness in performance assessment and increased consistency and reliability among managers in judging performance. Managers were able to make more accurate judgments about performance and recommend fair merit increases. We replaced the five performance appraisal categories, which ranged from 'outstanding performance to unacceptable performance', with six performance categories which would enable more accurate judgments of an individual's performance against the requirements of the role. The new rating categories asked the manager to judge where in the range of the role an individual was performing—in the top or bottom half of the role and at which of three steps in that half halves—high, mid or low.

The Manager-once-Removed (the manager's manager) reviewed the performance ratings and recommended merit increases prepared by his/her managers to ensure each was applying a standard, fair and accurate rating process to all employees.

Performance appraisals and merit increases, two highly emotionally charged issues, could now be handled more efficiently and effectively. Employees were fully aware that the changes in the compensation and performance management program meant the 'performance bar' had not been lowered but had been raised, and they agreed this exchange was fair.

The Requisite Principles and Roche Strategic Planning

The Requisite Organization principles had another important impact. Vic was interested in implementing Norton and Kaplan's Balanced Scorecard concept but wanted to ensure it was consistent with the Requisite Organization approach. He asked Elliott, Nancy and me to work out how to apply the Scorecard concept.

What needed to be worked out was how to apply the Scorecard concept in a multi-functional, multi-level organization.

The approach we developed strengthened the business planning process for managers who were already very adept at business planning. Scorecard deliverables or 'Key Goals' and 'Indicators' with targeted completion times appropriate for each organization level were developed. Goals were aligned and integrated, including appropriate time spans, from the level of the president down to the first organization level and horizontally across all functions. This process enabled every employee to have a 'Key Goals' card and see how his/her 'Key Goals' aligned with those at the next higher organization level. For example, function vice presidents working with the president were accountable for developing and achieving 'five year end goals or deliverables' which were integrated with the president's 'five year interim goals' which led to achievement of his '10 year vision' for the organization.

'Key Goals' would be updated annually or as dictated by events. A mid-course 'temperature reading' was planned for each six months. A periodic review of the Key Indicators would be used to reveal any deviations from course and determine satisfactory performance. In addition, the senior team would reflect upon the progress made and the soundness of the premises upon which the 'Key Goals' were set. Regardless of whether or not the Indicators showed progress to be on target, further reflection on emerging conditions and further changes might suggest that the original goals were too conservative, too optimistic, or in the wrong direction and therefore in need of modification.

The overall goal of the process was, of course, to ensure that every function and employee understood what individual and team contributions were necessary to help Roche Canada achieve its goals.

The comprehensive and scientific approach embodied in Requisite Organization to organization design and management provided Roche with a sharper understanding of the nature of the organization—just what sort of thing it is, how it is made up, how it functions, and some of the best ways of managing it. It added value by enhancing the decisions that depend upon or impact good organization and management. For example, Roche had better answers to questions such as:

- How do we retain our focus on customers, markets, and the competition?
- How can we better execute our strategies?
- What employee development investments will provide the greatest return for the company and the employee?
- How do we link our human resources to the company's strategy?

Requisite principles enabled Roche Canada to strengthen its organization structure, accurately assess employee capability, train and hold managers accountable for the best managerial practices, and clarify managerial and cross-functional accountabilities and authorities.

Lessons Learned at Roche Canada

I believe that many of the lessons learned at Roche Canada about organization and management could form part of the innovative and successful recovery strategies needed to address the continuing crisis in the pharmaceutical industry. While a wide variety of interdependent and complex solutions are necessary to steer the industry through a turbulent environment, one that has not been considered is a scientific and well-researched approach to organization and management.

The key lessons of organization and management for the pharmaceutical industry include:

1. Getting the number of organization levels right

Getting the number of organization levels right is paramount. Unless we got just the right number, sustainable organization growth and development would be greatly constrained.

2. Aligning organization levels and employee capability

Organization levels are categories of work complexity. The alignment of employee capability and compensation with these levels are necessary to obtain efficient and effective results and outcomes.

3. Alignment of the organization's spine

The correct number of vertical levels and the optimal grouping of functions form the backbone of the organization. Until the levels and groupings are optimal, all other initiatives will be sub-optimal (e.g., business planning, defining accountabilities and authorities, selection and development of employees, establishing and managing teams, etc.)

4. Vertical distance between managers and direct reports

Managers must be one level above the direct report in terms of capability and the level of complexity of work performed. When the relationship is too close, with manager and direct report working at the same organization level, the direct report is micro-managed and cannot use his/her initiative. When the relationship is too far apart, the manager feels the direct report lacks capability and initiative and the direct report feels the manager does not provide good context, direction and support for the work. Getting this working relationship right is the most powerful factor in organization structuring and design.

5. **Clear and common understanding of what it means to be a manager and clearly defined managerial accountabilities and authorities**

Effective understanding and implementation of these accountabilities and authorities ensure good governance, good leadership, and the development and maintenance of a trust-based organization.

6. **Clear cross-functional accountabilities and authorities**

Clear cross-functional accountabilities and authorities, rather than the vague and confusing definitions of 'dotted line or lateral relationships' and 'matrix organizations', are essential to reduce organization silos, 'turfs' and to create effective working relationships between functions, thus increasing the flow and quality of work across the organization.

The increasingly intense levels of interactions required between functions, corporate offices and country level affiliates and across the supply chain demands clear specification of accountabilities and authorities. Unclear accountabilities and authorities lead to extreme inefficiencies and acrimonious working relationships.

7. **Effective managerial leadership practices**

Capability or raw cognitive power is a necessary but not sufficient condition for effective managerial leadership. Clearly defined managerial leadership accountabilities, authorities and practices are essential for good organization governance and performance.

8. High-performing teams

Well-established project and coordinative teams can accomplish the intense collaborative work required within and between the major functions of organizations. To enable high performing teams requires:

- clear accountabilities and authorities for team leaders and members of both project and coordinative teams;
- clearly defined role relationships between teams and the rest of the organization;
- selection criteria and processes for team leaders and members;
- processes for delegation of authorities; and
- guidelines for applying human resource management policies—personal effectiveness appraisals, rewards and recognition, training and development, and other types of team support.

Summary

With good organization and management as one of its key initiatives, the pharmaceutical industry would be better positioned to regain credibility with customers, suppliers and other key stakeholders. The use of Requisite Organization principles and practices could provide a critical strategic resource to create the robust future for the industry which must be created because of its critical role in health care solutions.

Glossary

Accountability

Accountability is a situation where an individual can be called into account for his/her actions by another individual. See Managerial Accountability.

Aided Direct Output (ADO)

Aided Direct Output is Direct Output carried out with the assistance of subordinates. The subordinates are providing Direct Output Support (DOS).

Alignment

Alignment in an organization is getting the right function at the right level.

Association

An association is a social institution where the members of the group come together for a common purpose. There are non-voluntary associations, such as nations, whose citizens do not have free choice of membership. There are voluntary associations, such as companies, trade unions, and clubs in which the individuals have chosen to become members.

Authority

Authority is the power vested in a person by virtue of role to expend resources: financial, material, technical and human.

Business Unit

A business unit is a profit and loss account unit. It may stand alone or be within a corporation.

Capability

Capability is the ability of a person to do work.

Coaching

Coaching is the process through which a manager helps subordinates to understand the full range of their individual roles, what they need to do to perform the work of that role effectively, and what they need to do in order to develop in that role. The coaching of subordinates is an ordinary and necessary part of every manager's regular activities and an integral part of a manager's continuing review of each subordinate's personal effectiveness.

Complexity of Information Processing (CIP)

A person's complexity of information processing (CIP) is the complexity of mental activity a person uses in carrying out work. Complexity is determined by the number of factors, the rate of change of those factors and the ease of identification of the factors in a situation.

Compensation

The total remuneration granted to an employee in exchange for work and comprising all forms of payment including money and the financial equivalent of non-monetary payments.

Counseling

Counseling by the manager or Manager-once-Removed is done when someone asks for advice with a personal problem.

Cross Functional Working Relationship (CFWR)

Cross Functional Working Relationships are lateral or horizontal relationships that define the accountability and authority in a role in relations to other role(s) across functions. They are relationships in which A is authorized to initiate B's doing something but where it is B's manager and not A who is held accountable for whether or not B does it and for B's output. Dr. Jaques earlier called these Task Initiating Role Relationships (TIRRS). CFWRs include:

Advisory Accountability and Authority: A is accountable for providing advice to B and trying to persuade him/her to take the advice. B is accountable for deciding whether or not to take the advice and, if B decides not to, then A does nothing further.

Auditing Accountability and Authority: A is accountable for inspecting B's work and deciding if it is acceptable within prescribed limits. If it is not within limits B must stop until the matter is referred higher.

Collateral Accountability and Authority: A and B are subordinates of the same manager and are accountable for making mutual adjustments in their work so that the best over-all result is achieved in the light of the context set by their manager. If they cannot agree, they see their manager.

Coordinative Accountability and Authority: A has monitoring authority with respect to specified individuals and also has the authority to bring them together and try to persuade them to take a common course of action.

Monitoring Accountability and Authority: A is accountable for keeping abreast of what B is doing and for taking opportunities to persuade B to take alternative courses of action which A thinks might be better. If B does not accept A's persuasion and A considers the matter to be serious, then A must report to higher authority.

Prescribing Accountability and Authority: A has the authority to instruct B to carry out particular activities, and B is accountable for doing so, including carrying out the activities at the time prescribed.

Service-Getting and Service-Giving Accountability and Authority: The service-getter, A, has the authority to go to the service-giver, B, and to instruct B to provide an authorized service. B is accountable for providing the service unless s/he does not have the resources to do so, in which case B must indicate to A whether and when it will be possible to provide the authorized service.

Current Applied Capability (CAC)

Current Applied Capability is the capability someone has to do a certain kind of work in a specific role at a given level at the present time. It is a function of his/her complexity of information processing, how much s/he values the work of the role, his/her skilled use of knowledge for the tasks in the role, and the absence of temperamental characteristics that get in the way of getting work done.

Current Potential Capability (CPC)

Current Potential Capability is a person's highest current level of complexity of information processing. It determines the maximum level at which someone could work at the present time, given the opportunity to do so and provided that the work is of value to him/her, and given the opportunity to acquire the necessary skilled knowledge. This is the level of work that people aspire to have and feel satisfied if they can get. When people have work at their CPC, they feel they have an opportunity for the full expression of their potential.

Decision

The making of a choice with the commitment of resources.

Delegation

Delegation is the act of assigning a task to a subordinate.

Delegated Direct Output (DDO)

Delegated Direct Output is output which is assigned to be produced and sent out at subordinate levels.

Direct Output (DO)

Direct Output is output that is sent out directly by the individual producing it and not sent up for approval.

Direct Output Support (DOS)

Direct Output Support is the assistance a subordinate provides to a manager in completing the manager's own direct output.

Discretionary Content

The Discretionary Content of a task are those aspects of a task about which a subordinate must exercise his/her own judgment in order to fulfill the manager's instructions. Discretion always contains judgment with regard to both pace and quality of work to ensure that the work is done on time and to quality standards.

Equilibration

Equilibration is the balancing by managers of the standards being used by their immediate subordinate managers in appraising and managing their own immediate subordinates.

Equitable Pay Differentials

Equitable Pay Differentials are differences in payment between work at different levels that are experienced by the incumbents as fair and just.

Functions

Functions are main types of activity which are required by the objectives of an organization. There are functions that can be generalized for all managerial hierarchies. Functions must be aligned at each organizational level.

Future Potential Capability (FPC)

Future Potential Capability is the maximum level at which a person will be capable of working at some time in the future.

Gearing

Gearing for Talent Pool is the process whereby the Manager-once-Removed and immediate subordinate managers check their judgments with each other regarding the levels of current potential capability of individuals in the next two layers down.

General Responsibility

A General Responsibility is an instruction which applies indefinitely that specifies conditions which, whenever they arise, require an employee to make decisions or take actions within prescribed limits. The task content of a general responsibility lies in the activities that have to be carried through at the times prescribed. The content of these activities may sometimes be prescribed or may sometimes be left to the discretion of the subordinate.

Information Processing Methods

There are four methods of information processing that recur at different Orders of Information Complexity:

Declarative—reasoning by bringing forward a number of reasons that are separate with no connection made to any other reasons

Cumulative—reasoning by bringing together a number of different ideas

Serial—reasoning by constructing a line of thought made up of a sequence of ideas, each one of which leads to the next

Parallel—reasoning by examining a number of possible positions, each arrived at by means of serial processing that can be interlinked

Individual Contributor

An individual contributor is anyone who is mainly engaged in producing direct output. These persons do not delegate their work but complete the final output themselves. Individual contributors' work may occur at any level in the organization based on the level of work of the role. Individual contributors may be managers of subordinates who provide them with direct output support.

Induction

Induction is the process a manager uses to provide subordinates new to the role with the information necessary to do the work of that role.

Knowledge

Knowledge consists of facts, including procedures, that have been learned and can be reproduced.

Level of Work

The Level of Work in a role is the complexity of what needs to be done. This results in the weight of responsibility felt in that role. The level of work in any role can be measured by the time span of the longest tasks in that role.

Manager

A manager is a person in a role in which s/he is held accountable not only for his/her own personal effectiveness but also for the work and the working behavior of subordinates.

Managerial Accountability

The accountability managers have for their own personal effectiveness; the output of their subordinates; exercising effective managerial leadership of their subordinates; and, building and sustaining an effective team of subordinates capable of producing the assigned outputs.

Managerial Authority

A manager has the minimum authority with regard to immediate subordinates to decide: assignment of tasks, personal effectiveness appraisal, to veto the selection of an unsuitable candidate and to initiate removal from role of a subordinate judged not capable of the work of the role.

Managerial Hierarchies

Managerial Hierarchies are organizations used for employing people to get work done. They are employment systems organized into accountability hierarchies of manager and subordinate roles. It is a vertical organization for getting work done with clearly specified accountabilities.

Manager-once-Removed (MoR)

The manager of a subordinate's immediate manager is that subordinate's manager-once-removed.

Maturation

A maturation process is one in which a given aspect of a person is biologically innate and grows in a regular way to a predictable end state, so long as the individual does not encounter any severely limiting environmental conditions, especially in infancy.

Measurement

Measurement is the quantification of a property of an entity by means of an objective measuring instrument.

Mode

Mode is the highest level of Complexity of Information Processing to which an individual will finally mature.

Mentoring

Mentoring is a periodic discussion by a Manager-once-Removed to help a Subordinate-once-Removed to understand his/her potential and how that potential might be developed to achieve as full a career growth in the organization as possible.

Mutual Recognition Unit (MRU)

A mutual recognition unit is a unit which is small enough (under 250 people) for all of its members to be able to recognize one another.

Orders of Information Complexity

There are four methods of information processing that have been found to recur at higher and higher orders of complexity of the information that is being processed, giving a recursive hierarchy of categories.

Pre-Verbal—Expressed in infancy by gestures and physical contact with objects

Concrete Verbal—Thinking and language used in childhood tied to physical pointing out of things referred to that are present or have recently been present

Symbolic Verbal—The form of thinking and language used by most adults (Stratum I through IV) that does not have to have specific tangible items present but can represent them by symbols

Conceptual Abstract—Thought and language used at Stratum V and above that refers to other thoughts and words rather than to tangible things.

Universals—Thought and language used at Stratum IX and above to create new universal theories, new types of society, new systems of values, ethics, morality and culture.

Organization

Any system with an identifiable structure. The focus in this book is on employment organizations that are managerial hierarchies.

Assumed Organization—the pattern of connections between roles as it is assumed to be by the different individuals who occupy positions in the organization.

Extant Organization—the pattern of connections between roles as shown by systematic research to be actually operating.

Formal/Informal Organization—these terms are not used in this book; they are replaced by the concepts of manifest, assumed, extant, and requisite organization

Manifest Organization—The structure of an organization as it appears on the organization chart

Requisite Organization—the pattern of connections which ought to exist between roles if the system is to work efficiently and to operate as required by the nature of the work to be done and the nature of human nature.

Organizational Culture

Organizational Culture includes: rules and regulations; resources; customs and practices; shared values; language; belief systems; economics; policies and procedures; and traditions and assumptions.

Organization Process

Organization process consists of practices and procedures that enable the organization to function effectively.

Organizational Structure

Organizational structure is a system of roles and role relationships that people have when they work together. These role relationships establish the boundaries within which people relate to each other.

Output

Output is the product/service produced in a given period of time.

P, Pr and T

The three specialist staff functions are Personnel (P), programming (work flow and business modeling) (Pr) and production technology (T).

Project Team

A project team is an ad hoc group of individuals brought together under a team leader to complete a particular assignment. There is always a specific manager accountable for the team output.

Role

A role is a position within an organization.

Role Complexity

Role complexity is the complexity of tasks in a role as measured by time-span.

Role Relationships

Role relationships are connections between roles that define working relationships between individuals who occupy those roles in term of accountability, authority and content. Role relationships include both vertical task assigning relationships and cross functional working relationships.

Skill

A skill is an ability, learned through training, experience and practice, to carry out a given procedure without having to pay attention, i.e., what a person has learned to do without thinking through the steps involved.

Stratum (plural: Strata)

Managerial strata are organizational layers in a managerial hierarchy. The work in a given stratum is characterized by a specific range of complexity.

Subordinate-once-Removed (SoR)

The subordinate of a manager's immediate subordinate is that manager's subordinate-once-removed.

Talent Pool Development (TPD)

Talent Pool Development is a system for the development of a population of employees who have a distribution of current and future potential capability to discharge the company's current and future human resourcing requirements. The system includes talent pool mapping, selection, recruitment, mentoring, lateral transfers and other methods of individual career development.

Target Completion Time

The time a manager has in mind by when s/he needs a specific task to be completed.

Task

A task is an assignment to produce a specified output. Tasks have a specified quantity (Q) and quality (Q), and a targeted completion time (T) and are carried out with allocated resources (R) and within specified limits (policies and procedures). A manager assigns a **task** and the subordinate **works** to complete it. A task is a "what by when" or a QQT/R.

Task Assigning Role Relationships (TARRs)

Task Assigning Role Relationships are relationships in which A is not only authorized to get B to do something, but is also held accountable by his/her own manager for B's output (and its quantity, quality and delivery time, within resources and procedures). These are vertical role relationships.

Task Complexity

Task complexity is the complexity of information that has to be handled in carrying out a task. No measure of task complexity has yet been developed, yet managers have a good sense of the differences in complexity of tasks.

Task Initiating Role Relationships (TIRRs)

See Cross Functional Working Relationships

Teaching

The term **teaching** is used to describe the imparting of knowledge to individuals by lectures and discussions.

Temperament

Temperament is the tendency a person has to behave in given ways. Minus T (-T) refers to temperamental qualities in an individual that are dysfunctional in the sense of preventing that individual from carrying out the work required.

Time Horizon

The requisite method of quantifying an individual's potential capability by using the time span of the longest task he or she can handle.

Time Span

Time Span provides the level of work of a role in a simple, objective type of measurement of the weight of responsibility in that role. The longer the time span of a role, the higher is the level of complexity of the work in that role. The time span of a role is measured in terms of those tasks that have the longest target completion time as specified by the immediate manager of the role.

Training

The term training is used to describe the process of helping individuals to develop or enhance their skills through practice, either on the job or in learning simulations.

Values

Values are those things to which an individual will give priority or wants to do. Values direct our actions and enable commitment.

Work

Work is the exercise of judgment and discretion in making decisions in carrying out goal directed activities, that is in attempting to carry out a task.

CPSIA information can be obtained at www.ICGtesting.com
Printed in the USA
LVOW132343260313

326158LV00001B/62/A